W9-BTG-207

The Therapy Journal

The Therapy Journal

A Novel

by

Steven Wineman

Golden Antelope Press
715 E. McPherson
Kirksville, Missouri 63501
2017

Copyright ©2017 by Steven Wineman
Cover Design by by Russell Nelson
Cover Photos by Arkusha and Nadino (Shutterstock)

All rights reserved. No portion of this publication may be duplicated in any way without the expressed written consent of the publisher, except in the form of brief excerpts or quotations for review purposes.

ISBN   978-1-936135-37-0 (1-936135-37-X)

Library of Congress Control Number: 2017952495

Published by:
Golden Antelope Press
715 E. McPherson
Kirksville, Missouri 63501

Available at:
Golden Antelope Press
715 E. McPherson
Kirksville, Missouri, 63501
Phone: (660) 665-0273
http://www.goldenantelope.com
Email: ndelmoni@gmail.com

In memory of my parents, Jerry Pliscou Wineman and Dave
Wineman; and in memory of Elisabeth Morrison

Although Freud, claiming that 'we are never so defenseless against suffering as when we love,' pursues the line of defense as it leads through anger and conscience to civilization and guilt, the more interesting question would seem to be why the mother is willing to take the risk.

—Carol Gilligan, *In a Different Voice*

Every story is a story about death.

—Helen Humphreys, *The Lost Garden*

*But one voice got through, caught her up by surprise
It said, 'Don't hold us back, we're the story you tell.'*

—Dar Williams, "You're Aging Well"

Please note that this book includes explicit descriptions of sex trafficking and child sexual abuse.

Contents

Part I

Therapy

My name is Becky. I'm eight years old. I live deep inside the big body of a woman. She says that her name is Becky too. But I call her Fucking Bitch.

I know I'm only eight and I'm not supposed to use words like that, only grown-ups get to swear, grown-ups and fucking teenagers but not when you're a nice little girl. Well I am not a nice little girl, which you're probably already getting the idea. I don't really give a fuck what I'm supposed to be or not supposed to be, what I'm supposed to say or not say. No one pays the least bit of attention to me anyway so what does it matter. I'm just a little girl and I'm all alone.

Here's a good one. The Fucking Bitch is a *therapist*. Can you believe it? All day long people come and spill their guts out to her and think she could actually help them. She sits there in her pleated woolen over-the-knee skirts and nods and has this serious look on her face and says stuff like "I hear you saying bladdy blah" and she's so fucking phony I hardly know what to do with myself. I mean they even pay her *money*. I am not making this shit up.

The worst thing is that I have to listen to all the crap that comes out of their mouths, and sometimes they cry and I have to listen to that too, can you imagine? The real point is, who the fuck listens to me? Who listens to all the crap that comes out of *my* mouth? Who listens to me cry? Who sits with me in a pleated wool skirt wearing a serious expression on her face and says, "I'm hearing you say bladdy blah"? NOBODY, that's fucking who.

One

I knew I was pregnant the second I woke up, a sharp undeniable knowing that penetrated my hangover blur and I thought, *I've done this to myself.* Doctors will tell you it's impossible to feel anything so early, that there are no physical signs until the fetus implants in the uterus. But there it was, a new life inside my body.

I felt the man's presence and then turned my head and looked at him, lying on his back with one arm splayed out away from me, his breath slow and even, a face full of stubble. Do men have any idea what it's like to wake up next to them in the morning, how repulsive they are? In that instant I told myself, he will never know. It didn't feel like a choice, already an accomplished fact.

I pulled my body out of bed, walked slowly and calmly to the bathroom and vomited into the toilet. The alcohol, I told myself. I couldn't remember how much I drank. Much too soon for morning sickness. The rational mind.

I walked back down the hallway a little unsteady on my feet and when I got to the doorway of my bedroom I turned and there he was—where else would he be?—but still the sight of him was jarring; he had rolled toward the center of the bed and now he was on his side, clutching the pillow with one hand, the outline of his legs scissored beneath the crumpled topsheet, blankets pushed and dangling over the side, and I hated how he had made the bed his. Clothes were strewn across the floor in front of me, chinos, jeans, a yellow tee, a navy blue tee, his plaid flannel shirt, jockey shorts, garish dark green socks, a plain white bra, lacy black panties. Last night's debris. I navigated my way one careful step at a time until I reached the closet where I found a robe.

In the kitchen I made coffee and waited. I don't know how much time passed. I was in a kind of trance. I sat there and sipped coffee and watched myself, this pregnant woman, this slipping of a life from one state of being to another. I looked down at the surface of my kitchen table and lost myself in the texture of the grain, shifting tones of blond and brown, lines curving in gentle arcs, wood that was once alive. The coffee was bitter and I let it go cold, I shivered in my thin robe, my head throbbed. I knew I was spacing out and at the exact same time, outside my field of vision, beneath random thoughts and physical sensations I was anchored in the certainty that the man lying in my bed was a stranger and whatever monumental thing was happening inside my body, he had nothing to do with it. *Fucking prick, fucking prick, fucking prick*, from out of nowhere the words filled my mind like a chant and I thought, I'm not having an integrated response to this.

Finally he walked in, dressed, his shirt crumpled, managing to look smug and self-absorbed and I felt myself pull even further away from him if that was possible. In a subdued voice, which was not actually sad but could be taken that way if he wanted to, I said, "You know, George, I don't think this is working out."

Interesting to note that I'm not repulsed by my male clients. They come to me like little boys—that's a line in a Joni Mitchell song but it's true. Some of them are open about it, there's a kind of coming out that happens once they feel safe with me, once there's enough trust and they can say in effect, look, don't be fooled by this shell of a man, this big hulking body; here is who I really am and who I really am is small and frightened and all alone in the world. Well, some of these guys, if you saw them on the street you wouldn't think of them as big or hulking but that's their psychological reality, the male script. That's who they've learned they are supposed to be and it's who they know they're not.

Other men don't ever shed the script, they're like snakes stuck in their dead and useless skins. Those are the ones who don't really know why they come to me, who have partners saying go to therapy or I'm leaving, or who have had their lives fall apart and now are trying to put themselves back together without any clue about what really happened or what putting themselves together would actually mean. Or occasionally I'll get referrals from courts for men in legal trouble who've had therapy ordered as a condition for probation. Men who sit in my office and go through litanies of all the others who are to blame for their troubles, who shift their weight from side to side and won't make eye contact and clear their throats and deflect my questions. But they don't repulse me either. Maybe the point is that I can see their little boys, feel their presence in the room.

Of course I don't go to bed with my male clients, I don't have to wake up next to them in the morning.

So I've learned to sit with men and hear their stories, to find some core of humanity in them and some place in me capable of compassion. But it's the women I see who break my heart. Not all of them, of course, there are women as defended as the toughest men. But the ones who dissolve into their most aching primitive selves, the ones who have been violated in places beyond words—and it's not just what they have gone through, the devastation, things my profession reduces to clinical jargon like posttraumatic stress disorder, major depression, bipolar disorder, all in the service of keeping our distance—sometimes I listen to them and I see their faces, the horror of their lives throbbing right there in front of me, and in some of those moments I don't keep my distance. They take me, these women, to a knowledge of the human condition, not just what they have gone through but what has been done to them, done to them by human beings, something I'm not always sure I want to know.

I waited two weeks until my period was officially late, then got a drugstore pregnancy test which came out positive, as I had known it would. I followed up with a test at my primary care clinic, also positive.

The HIV test would have to wait for three months.

I hadn't touched alcohol or pot since the day I conceived, the obvious precaution but it didn't mean I'd decided to keep the child, only that I was leaving my options open.

This came up when I had dinner with my parents, not pregnancy but alcohol. It would have been the moment to say it, when my father offered me a glass of wine and I refused, but telling my parents that I was pregnant was the last thing on my mind. I was sitting in the living room of their house in Newton and Dad ambled in carrying two glasses, mine already poured and why wouldn't it be, it was a ritual that extended back for two decades, sharing a glass of wine before dinner and eking out what space we could from my mother's presence that so much filled the house. Mom labored in the kitchen, having waved away my offer to help, and the walls of that sturdy house will crumble before my father lifts a finger to prepare anything more complicated than a peanut butter sandwich. I know that sounds bitter but it wasn't how I felt at the time; I was aware of my father's shortcomings but I had always thought they were outweighed by his strengths, his affection, his genuine interest in my work, his acceptance of me as my own person living my life. All this in contrast to my mother, the benchmark against which I measured my father, and I cut him a lot of slack for being a man of his generation whose place was not the kitchen, for his attitudes about women, his drinking. The bitterness would come later.

I sat there feeling oppressed as I always did by the dark colors in the living room, the maroon chair I was sitting in, two more matching chairs, wine red, the deep green of the couch, thick wall to wall carpeting, also green. A large rectangular mirror occupied the wall above the sofa, something I had taken for granted when I was growing up but as an adult every time I look at it I think, who has a mirror on their living room wall? The mantel below the mirror was crammed with my mother's tchotchkes, plastic animals, a little stuffed skunk, a monkey, masks of various sizes, a set of Russian dolls lined up smallest to biggest, an assortment of trinkets, a ceramic laughing Buddha with an exposed round belly. Next to me there was a round table with a mosaic tile top, in the middle of the table a sleek mahogany wading bird. To one side of the bird was a photo of me, age six with a big smile, a dimple on each cheek, missing a front tooth, dark hair braided into pigtails tied with soft red ribbons—a cheerful little girl, her gaze fixed on something just left of the camera. To the other side a photo of my brother Mark, older, in middle school I would guess, wearing a dark jacket and white shirt with button down collar and tie, hair combed back off his forehead, staring straight ahead, his expression serious and flat and very male.

Dad approached and extended one of the wineglasses toward me. He's a highly regarded child psychologist, semi-retired, having closed his practice two years ago but still much sought after as a consultant and speaker. An elegant white haired man with his neatly trimmed mustache, impeccably dressed in a blue jacket and necktie in his own home on a Sunday evening for no reason other than his love of fine clothing and proper appearance. What my mother would deride as his narcissism. "Here you are, Becky," he said, and I said, "No thanks, Dad," trying to sound casual but I felt my heart beating, the shiver in my lower lip and he looked at me and just perceptibly lifted an eyebrow. "No?" he said. "No," I said, "not tonight, Dad. I don't feel like it." He looked again, the question poised on his tongue. Then he gave a little shrug and put both glasses down on the table by the end of the couch where he lowered himself, leaving it unasked. I felt the space taken up between us by this information I was withholding, and at the same time I loved him so much for letting me be with it.

A minute later I heard my mother calling from the kitchen, "Rebecca!"

Rebecca. Since I was eight years old I have been Becky. For thirty fucking years I had been telling my mother to call me Becky, and for thirty fucking years she had been refusing. It was a proxy war between us, a struggle over which of us got to define me, and every single time it was my mother's statement that she would never see me for who I really am. I heard her piercing voice with its usual twinge of desperation; my body clenched and I asked myself why in the hell I kept stepping foot into her house.

When I was five I was hit by a car. That's how we always described it afterward though the truth is I've never known whether the car actually touched me. I wasn't hurt, just scared from all the uproar that anyone, let alone a five year old, would feel sitting in the street and staring into a bumper that's inches from your face, the bumper attached to something you know could have crushed you. But even that was cushioned and softened by all the attention I got, from everyone and especially my mother telling me over and over that I was fine, the feeling that I was special and that everyone who mattered was paying attention to me and being extra nice, my mother and father and the driver of the car and neighbors from the houses on both sides of us and the nurses and doctor at the emergency room. So it ended up being an adventure.

It happened on a Saturday morning. My mother was down in the basement doing laundry and I don't know where my father was, or my brother. But I was in the living room watching a cartoon when I got the idea to go visit Cynthia, the seven year old who lived across the street. I idolized her and all I could think was how great it would be to ring her doorbell and surprise her, and then maybe she would let me come in and we could play with dolls or bake cookies or lie on the floor and watch her TV. I opened our front door and walked out onto the porch; it was a sunny fall day, a little chilly and I wondered if I should go back in for my jacket but I could see Cynthia's house on the other side of the street and I would only be outside for a very short time so I kept going, down our steps and walkway to the sidewalk. I crossed the sidewalk and went into the street, my dad's car was parked there, it was a dark blue Toyota Corolla and I was proud of myself for knowing what kind it was. I walked right by it and didn't look both ways so it was really all my fault. My eyes were glued on Cynthia's front door and I couldn't wait to get over there and then I heard the screeching sound to my left, it was really loud and coming toward me and I turned and looked and saw the car and I wanted to get out of its way but I didn't know which way to go so instead I froze, and the next thing I knew I was on my bum on the pavement and the screeching sound had stopped and the car's black bumper was inches from my face.

The driver of the car, a woman with a blond ponytail and glasses and a blue windbreaker—she was standing over me in a flash and then she was kneeling down, she was crying and trying to say things and it was all garbled but I got that she felt really bad and somehow it made me feel better that she was so upset. Then my mother was with me and I never even saw her coming, it was like one second I was trying to understand what the woman from the car was saying and the next second my mom was sitting right down on the pavement with me and she had me wrapped up in her arms and I buried my face in her shirt. It was maroon and soft and pillowy and had a Mom smell I would know anywhere. She was telling the woman that she was sure I would be okay and nothing seemed broken and just look, I was conscious and sitting up and she knew it wasn't the woman's fault and she was so so so grateful the woman had stopped in time. Then Mom asked me if anything hurt and I tried to answer but now I was the one who was garbled because I was talking into her shirt; she laughed and said Honey you need to move your face so I can understand you. So I did, I sat back up but her arms were still around me and my hands were on her sides and I said my bum hurt a little from when I fell on it and she said did anything else hurt and I said no. She looked right in my eyes and smiled her big smile and said Rebecca you're going to be just fine. I rested my head on her chest again and I felt so safe with her holding me like that.

Looking at my mother as I know her now, a brittle needy woman who can be overwhelmed by almost anything beyond her control, it's hard to believe she wasn't helplessly hysterical when she found me on the pavement inches from having been run over, that she didn't start screaming at the driver and panic about me being hurt and make me feel with her reaction that everything was coming unglued. But at the time I knew her through the eyes and heart of a little girl. She was just my mom, the person I depended on more than anyone else in the world, and I wasn't thinking about anything except that she was there and I was okay.

Afterward it became a family legend, The Day Rebecca Was Hit By The Car and I can trace my relationship with my mother by how I reacted during the many times she told the story over the years. When I was little I loved it, I thought it was all about me and I was the heroine with the happy ending. By the time I was nine or ten I began to notice that it was really more my mother who was the heroine, how she heard the screech of the tires and came rushing out to the street and wrapped her little girl in her loving arms and somehow managed to calm down the hysterical woman and just all around saved the day. As I got older it seemed like she embellished it with every telling. She would play up how scared I was but it had all happened too fast for me to get as scared as she was saying. Then she had me crying my eyes out when she got to me, and I'm certain I wasn't crying even a little. I would try to tell her and she would say, Oh honey, you just don't remember how upset you were. Later she added a whole new wrinkle, claiming that my father was supposed to be watching me while she was down doing the laundry, making him out to be the villain. If Dad was there he would shrug and roll his eyes, sometimes he got a grin out of me but mostly it pissed me off that Mom had to blame him for everything. Finally I just didn't want to hear it, I felt like she had taken something sweet and turned it into poison, I would say Jesus, Mom, how many times can you tell the same story? and walk away.

Sometimes I call her FB, you know that's short for Fucking Bitch. Not because I think or I feel or I have any kind of whatever you want to call it about swearing. It's just easier to call her FB, she's not even worth the time and the effort it takes to say the whole words. But I know what it means and it's still a fucking swear because that's what she deserves and that's what she is, a Fucking Bitch.

She acts like I don't even exist. She thinks I grew up right along with her, just to show you what an ignoramus she is, as if I was that stupid little five year old who got hit by the car. I was NEVER five years old, I was nothing at all, just thin air until she was eight and then IT happened and poof! there I was. She doesn't know the first thing about me and I know everything about her. I'm like Santa Claus, I know when she's been sleeping, I know when she's been fucking, yes I do know what that means and I'm only eight and I'm not supposed to know about these things but if that was really true then whoever has arranged for my life didn't know what they were doing or should have given it just a little more thought.

Now the poor thing has gone and gotten herself pregnant. Well, I say good luck to her. Anyway, what's it got to do with me? Nothing, that's what. I mean why she would want Georgy Porgy or any man for that matter to stick his fucking prick into her is beyond me. It's disgusting and she even encouraged him, she actually put her *hand* on it and got it all hard and then look at what happened. Play with fire and you get burnt, that's what the adults always say and she is an adult so she ought to fucking know. Well she knows now. If I sound unkind it's because I am unkind. What else would you expect, I'm a piece of shit. And anyway, what difference does it make? I could say all the kind words in the English language and she wouldn't hear a single one of them.

Two

For ten years I saw a woman from Laos. We were the same age, twenty-eight, when she started with me. At first she was too raw to tell more than bits and pieces of her past but in time she felt safe enough to connect dots and her story came into focus.

Her given name was Lathsamy, and then after her oldest brother took her across the border to Thailand and sold her to a sex trafficking ring, they called her Lulu. She was nine. Three years later, a john rented her for the night, an American in Bangkok on business. When he saw her malnourished, undeveloped body he must have realized that she was still a little girl. He had something like an Amazing Grace moment, managed to get her to a safe haven run by a local advocacy group. Back in the States, he brokered an international adoption that brought her to a family in New Jersey. The man himself lived in the West but stayed in touch with the adoptive parents and the girl, visited when business brought him East, became a sort of uncle.

Her American name was Laura. When I met her, she was in her first year at Harvard Law School. A slender woman with a round face and long straight black hair, her body very taut, burning black eyes. She spoke flawless, precise English with a hint of New Jersey in her accent. A brilliant young person who had almost unimaginably overcome the obstacles of her origin, having arrived in this country illiterate, frightened, and disoriented, and climbed to the pinnacle of accomplishment. An inspiration, a poster child.

During her first semester at Harvard, Laura's life unraveled. Her benefactor had told the adoption agency and later her American family that he found her begging on the streets of Bangkok, abandoned by her family, sleeping in alleys. Once she was in the States, Laura heard this version of her history so often, spoken with such conviction, that she herself came to believe it was true. But the elite law school, the intense pressure to perform, the brutal methods of professors interrogating students in class must have pierced whatever mechanism was shielding her from her history. Laura had a sexual encounter with a man, and afterward lost pieces of her childhood started coming back. First she remembered her village in Laos, the faces of her parents, words and phrases spoken to her, fragments of a forgotten language. Then being taken to Thailand by her brother, his hard grip on her small arm, her bafflement and later the unreal terror of being left with strangers who took absolute control of her life. She remembered chaotic successions of men and rooms in Bangkok, images and physical sensations, the actual feel of hands holding her down, the heavy weight of bodies, penises stabbing her, moments of gagging, the constriction of her throat so present that she had to gasp for air. Odors of alcohol and bodies and semen. She remembered learning not to feel, how to leave her body. Finally she remembered her benefactor, the place where she met him, not begging on the street as she had been told so often but a hotel room, dimly lit, one more man, one more room, one more big naked body above her. She remembered, before the moment when whatever grace it was moved him to take her away from that life, how he fucked her.

She couldn't stop the memories. She couldn't eat. She couldn't sleep. There was no one she could possibly tell. At Thanksgiving Laura went to New Jersey, to a place she now understood had never been her home. She looked at her "parents" and they were strangers standing on the other side of a chasm there was no way to cross. She went back to school and changed her email account, changed her phone number, told no one. She lived in terror of her "uncle" coming to see her, finding her, having to see his face again, having to stand in any kind of proximity to his physical body. The word she used in her head for what he did to her was rape. It was a word that exploded across her life. She started to cut herself. She finished the semester, passed her exams, and checked herself into a psychiatric hospital.

I started working with her after she got out of the hospital that first time, ten years ago. She asked in a small voice if I could call her Lathsamy and except for one terrible summer several years later, that was how I always knew her, by her birth name. Two days out of the hospital she was a brittle frightened woman, barely able to say a few words without breaking down. She would tell fragments of stories, memories of her village, images from the three years in Bangkok; sometimes she would get through the description of a setting, a person, an event, sometimes only a few words before her face collapsed and her body shook and she couldn't speak. Little by little she told me about being a girl in Laos, living a normal life, a time of taking things for granted that would become tokens of a lost paradise—the touch of her mother's hand on her forehead, a man on a riverbank wearing a lampshade hat and pulling a net out of the river, the net full of thrashing fish. There were no narratives from Bangkok, only still frames of horror.

All I really did in those early days was listen to Lathsamy, and believe her, and through that come to believe in her. Not so hard if you let yourself become oriented in a certain way, like bending to the light, the radiant truth of another person's pain.

Or so I believed at the time. Knowing what I know now, given all that has happened, it couldn't have been so pure, the connection I thought I had with Lathsamy. The truth is I'm not sure how much I know, even now.

Who was I at twenty-eight? An idealistic young therapist, two years out of graduate school, who believed she could take her training and shape it into something better than a conventional practice, more compassionate, more human. I wanted to hold the best of what I had learned and jettison the crap, transcend all the ways that we use professional distance to shield ourselves from the full raw truths of human suffering. I so much wanted to believe in my clients, and I don't say this to deride myself or my idealism. It was wonderful as far as it went, I'm even willing to say that I as a therapist was wonderful as far as I went. It's just that I didn't go anywhere near as far as I thought I did.

The full raw truth. There was so much I didn't know about myself ten years ago. Now, looking back, I think that I couldn't really know the full truth of Lathsamy's pain, of anyone's, when there was so much of my own pain that I didn't know.

Who would have thought that Lathsamy as I first knew her, just out of the hospital, so fragile that it seemed all she could do was to get through one day and then the next, who would have thought she could go on to graduate from law school, pass the bar, launch her career as an attorney, marry and have a child? Who would have thought she could navigate through the terror of her recovered experience, the overwhelming betrayals and losses, so many fragments of identity and come out where she did on the other end?

Recovery from trauma. There are things we know, the need of survivors to tell their stories, the importance of safety and validation, the tendency to reenact traumatic events. We know that most victims, especially children, lack the ability to process terrible events when they occur, that in many cases it is not until years later that they are able to fully, to consciously, experience what has happened to them. We know the kind of psychological disintegration that happens when people are completely overpowered, their capacities to cope overwhelmed, when they lose access to instinctive responses of fight and flight. We know that regaining the ability to act, to make conscious choices and step out of the traumatized state of abject helplessness—we know that this is essential to recovery.

But how much do we actually know about resilience? I remember reading about a group of school children who were kidnapped and then left alone in an underground vault, until one boy found a passage out and led the others to safety. What made that boy different, able to act?

For three years of childhood Lathsamy was reduced to a subhuman state. If a single traumatic incident can cause lifelong damage, what are the consequences of hundreds of traumas on a young life?

She reverted to her birth name, not just with me but with everyone. Then she started from time to time to wear sinhs, the traditional tube skirts worn by Laotian women. These were immediate things she could do, choices she could make, and I thought they were ways of saying to herself that she was a different person than the one whose life in the States had been built on the wiping away of her history.

But who was this different person? Within the first few months of our working together she came to a session with a short piece of writing to show me, handwritten in her small precise script, black ink on plain white paper.

> *Identity, the clinical term. A legal principle (or legal fiction?) might use the Latin, identitatem. To clothe it in gravitas. But here I am. Not in class. Not in a casebook. Not in Laos, not in Bangkok. Not in Cherry Hill, not anywhere. Not clothed. Certainly not naked.*
>
> *This facility with words that aren't mine. This language I wear like borrowed skin. Borrowed from whom? On what terms? When the loan comes due, what then?*
>
> *This sinh I wear, not clothing. A costume.*
>
> *This name I wear, Lathsamy. Identitatem? Lathsamy Lathsamy Lathsamy. Or only a wish?*

She found a tutor to teach her Lao and learned that the fragments of language she had retrieved from her childhood were actually Thai.

She discovered there are many languages spoken in Laos, that Lao is only the official one, and there was no way to tell which language she was raised with as a little girl. Many languages and also many cultures, and no telling which culture had been hers. Behind these realizations came others. She knew appallingly little about her country of origin; her family in New Jersey—she would not use the word "parents" to describe them—had done nothing to help her learn about her heritage. Even if they falsely believed that she was Thai, which she understood was not their fault, she knew as little about Thailand as she did about Laos. Despite all the memories of Bangkok and scenes of abuse, the fragments of language, despite the images of her village and her true family, the name of her village in Laos remained a blank, and her family's name also a blank, so there was no way from the States to trace her family and find out who she had been as a little girl.

We spent many sessions talking about whether Lathsamy should go to Laos to search for her origins. It was possible. Over the summer she could spend up to two months there; she was on full scholarship at Harvard, and with savings from the years when she had worked before law school she could afford the trip. But once there what could she possibly hope to find with so little to go on? What might be gained just from making the effort? From actually being there, with opportunities to reconnect to her history, opportunities that were only possible in Laos? What were the psychological risks of being alone so far away in the thick of her history? The psychological costs of going and failing to find her family?

These were the questions that turned out to be too obvious, and ultimately not useful. Gradually Lathsamy realized that she was less frightened of not finding her family than she was of finding them. Only when she was able to visualize herself actually there with them, able to let go of the challenges of the search, and able to picture introducing herself to the woman who had stroked her forehead, the man by the river with the lampshade hat, the brother whose hand had gripped her arm—only then could she project the terror she would feel at actually facing these people, terror and rage and the reality of losses that could not be undone. Her brother who had done this to her, how could she possibly face him? And her parents—what if they knew? What if they were the ones who had made the decision, instructed their son to take his little sister across the border and sell her into slavery in Thailand? How could they have done such a thing? They might have been desperate, starving, maybe they had unthinkably horrible options to choose from. Maybe they were bad people. Or maybe they didn't know. Had they been grieving the loss of their daughter for these last twenty years?

How could she know? Not by sitting in my office, allowing herself to think and envision and most important to feel what it might be like to find them. But once she was there, even then how could she know? If she found her parents, if they told her that one day she vanished and they never knew what happened, how could she be sure? Isn't that what they would say regardless of the truth? By the look in their eyes, by their tears, by the feel of their bodies against hers as they embraced her, was that how she could tell? Could she trust her ability to discern their true feelings? To discern her own? Trust, the thing most basic between a child and her parents, how could this possibly be restored?

In the end Lathsamy chose not to go to Laos.

She also chose not to confront her "uncle." For Lathsamy this seemed an easy decision, if anything at that time could be called easy for her. All she wanted was the safety of keeping him out of her life.

But I found myself wondering about that man, an American on a business trip who would pay for sex apparently without qualms, certainly no qualms large enough to keep him from culminating the act—and then found himself so flooded with remorse that he spent months and eventually years of his life trying to make up for what he had done (with some convenient altering of the facts). What in his psyche could possibly have led him to such a reversal? A guy with a wife and two kids back in the States who suddenly looked at himself through his wife's eyes and was repulsed beyond what he could live with? Did he have a daughter Lathsamy's age? Had he been vacillating for years, committing unspeakably vile acts, then feeling overcome with shame and guilt? Or was he just a scumbag through and through who had one unaccountable burst of humanity?

I'll never know and I certainly wasn't going to raise any of this with Lathsamy. These were my questions, not hers, and my job as her therapist was to know the difference between my curiosity and her needs.

Lathsamy did ask her adoptive parents, the New Jersey couple, to come up to Cambridge and meet with her and me. She told them very little in advance, only that she was going through major changes with the help of a therapist and wanted to talk to them about it.

They walked into my office looking baffled, the man heavyset and balding, the woman with delicate features, wrinkles at the edges of her eyes, her blond hair the color it might once have been naturally. As they sat down the man glanced at the diploma framed in thin metal and mounted on the wall over my desk, Rebecca Hoffman, Master of Social Work, Boston University, and next to it my license to practice psychotherapy. The small desk occupied one corner of the office. On the opposite wall a single window with thin white curtains let in the soft light of late afternoon. Four chairs filled most of the open space. Lathsamy sat beside me and we faced the couple, so close that I could hear the rattling of the man's breath.

Speaking with a quiet contained dignity, Lathsamy told them her story. Not really a confrontation, more than anything it was a coming out. The man fidgeted, shifted his weight, averted his eyes. The woman held her hand over her mouth. At one point Lathsamy paused to take a breath, and the woman said, "Laura, sweetie, how could we have known?"

But when she comes to the part about breaking down and being hospitalized, the atmosphere in the room changes. "Oh you poor thing," the woman says. The subtext is impossible to miss, as if the unspoken words were projected onto a screen: How terrible, what a relief, she's *crazy*.

It is the one time Lathsamy silently loses her composure, her eyes flashing at me with a pleading rage. I tell the couple it is real, the sex slave trade, that it goes on to this day. I tell them I believe Lathsamy, that she needs to be believed. The man blinks, shakes his head as if trying to clear it. The woman, at a loss, says again, "You poor thing."

They left my office, the New Jersey couple, and Lathsamy stayed. After the door had closed she looked at me and said in a clear firm voice, "You see what they are, Becky. You see what I am. I'm an orphan."

She started to call them her nonparents. Her encounter with them opened a door that she walked through into a state of grief. What the New Jersey couple were not, what they had never been and could not possibly have replaced—recognizing these things enabled Lathsamy to see and to feel the depth of having lost her Laotian parents, the unbearable sadness of even referring to them that way, not just as "my parents"—the only parents she'd ever had, and now they were as lost to her as if they had died. For all she knew they could have died in the intervening years; the rupture had happened twenty years earlier, but now it had the finality to her of death. The irony was that during the long years of adolescence and early adulthood she had come to terms with the loss of her unknown, unremembered, supposedly Thai parents—believed she had come to terms, but in truth she had never grieved them.

Now she looked back with a kind of horror at how easily she had accepted the story of a life with no history, no childhood, at how little curiosity, how little feeling she had allowed herself about her place and self of origin. As the false story crumbled, she saw her persona in the narrative, Laura, as a false self, the born again American, the wunderkind, the daughter of kind and loving parents who provided her with so much she could never have had as a street urchin in Bangkok. The truth, devastating and overwhelming as it was, for a brief time also seemed to offer her a glimpse of things that could be regained, her true home, her true parents, her true self. Then that story fell apart too, leaving her with what?

She could feel, she could make choices; at bottom those were the things she was left with. She sobbed through many of our sessions and I tried to hold her with loving acceptance, not physically of course, I kept that professional boundary, but emotionally and even more so spiritually. It was a way of meeting her eyes, holding my own presence, speaking in soft gentle tones that conveyed, more in manner than words, that her feelings were exactly right, that I was not frightened by their intensity, and that my office was a place of safety where she could express everything she needed to express.

Gone was the sense that she was breaking down. In its place I felt that she was finding what was real inside herself, a kind of menagerie that to be sure included irretrievable losses, but also some kind of sea bed beneath all those horrors. I told her this. I talked to her about what it meant, her act of choosing to see me week after week, how she was affirming her own capacity to express her feelings, her choice to keep living, the possibilities that still existed in her life for safety and human connection.

She listened quietly when I would say these things, met my eyes and gave quick little nods. But later she brought me another piece of paper, a kind of written response.

> *Pain is real. There are many slippery slopes. My pain is an anchor. A red line across my arm. It was a red line across my arm. Now something inside. Becky says I have a sea bed. Which fits with the anchor, but. Metaphors don't matter at the end of the day. What matters? I feel. I bleed. I remember. I cry salt tears, salt of the earth. Salt of the roiling sea. I am supposed to be these things. I. I. I.*
>
> *Becky has such hopes for me. Together we have created a self. Will the self live up to Becky's hopes? Am I allowed*

to hope for this self?

But hope seems beside the point. Yes, I choose to see Becky every week. I choose to keep living. I choose to attend the Great Harvard Law School. I choose to excel in my studies. I choose these things, it must be true. I do these things so I must choose them. But.

Now where are the words? In English, in Lao, in Thai. Down on the ocean floor it is not me choosing these things. Not I. No words down there. No choices.

I asked Lathsamy if she felt I was imposing my hopes on her. "It's not that," she said.

"Then what?"

"Hope is beside the point for me," she answered quietly. "But not for you."

I thought it was fine, this difference between us that was not a disagreement. It seemed to me appropriate I should hold hope for Lathsamy that she was not ready to hold for herself. What else would a therapist do, if not believe in her client's future?

Alongside her grief, Lathsamy found ways to cope. She told me that at law school she knowingly hid behind the stereotype of the reserved, high-achieving young Asian woman, prepared and razor sharp in class, the rest of the time studying intently in a library carrel, polite but with little to say to her classmates. She kept on learning Lao, having decided it was the thing most readily at hand to provide some link to her origins, whether or not it was the language she had spoken as a child. She explored Eastern spirituality, starting with religions practiced in Laos, which led her to study different forms of Buddhism. The one she found herself most drawn to, for reasons she accepted without trying to understand, was Nichiren Buddhism, its roots in Japan but now practiced around the world. She set up a scroll called the Gohonzon in her apartment, chanted *nam-myoho-renge-kyo* every morning and evening, and joined a study group with people from many cultures where she formed bonds that over time would become a backbone for her recovery.

I went to Lathsamy's graduation from Harvard. I beamed, I cried, and though we were the same age I felt like a proud mother. I thought that Lathsamy was the most courageous person I had ever known.

Three

I was measuring time in weeks since conception and as the first weeks passed, I wasn't getting any closer to a decision. There was an eerie normalcy to my life, so much of my time and energy devoted to other people's problems, the rest spent in my usual routines. It might have helped if my body were sending me pregnancy signals—tender breasts, cramping, quease, anything; but the only pains I had were in the usual places, my head and shoulders, ordinary signs of stress. After that first surge of unaccountable physical knowing, some kind of disconnect was happening; I recognized it but I didn't understand it. Many things were beyond my understanding. I didn't talk to my friends about being pregnant and I didn't know why. I couldn't picture myself as a mother, I couldn't imagine ending a life. At thirty-eight this wasn't exactly my last chance but it was a chance, here for the taking. On the other hand if I was going to abort I'd rather do it with pills, time was running out for that and I could barely hold the thought. I couldn't see a path toward clarity, and then my attention would wander, dinner to make, the TV carelessly flipped on, and hours later I would realize that I had let myself forget about this decision that was hanging suspended somewhere, not being made, needing to be made.

The Friday of Week Five fell in the middle of October. My office is in North Cambridge and at the end of the day I walked home along a bike path that runs from Alewife Station into Somerville, where I live near Davis Square. The air hinted at a chill that sharpened when the wind blew in gusts, the last of the sun was slanting from the northwest, my favorite weather of the year. Foliage along the path was in full display, yellow, orange, red. People passed on bikes, on foot, a few with dogs on leashes, the usual array but it was an effort for me to take them in, I had nothing left and I couldn't read their expressions, the way they moved their bodies, and I felt very alone. I thought, *When have I not been alone? Everything else is window dressing, this is what's real.*

I got home wanting so badly to pour myself two fingers of vodka, a habit at the end of my work week. I thought of Lathsamy, who for years had been my last appointment on Friday, by design because I knew how much she took out of me. The accumulated stress from all of my week, my own predicament, random memories of Lathsamy, these things tangled together in the fatigue of a late Friday afternoon, in the yearning for a drink I couldn't have. I give and give to people all week and I just wanted something for myself.

That was when it popped into my head: what would I, as a therapist, say to someone, a client, coming to me presenting (as we say) what I myself was presenting? A thirty-eight year old woman, single, pregnant, apparently overwhelmed, unable to decide whether to keep the child or end the pregnancy. What would I tell her? How would I help her? What would I say to myself?

I pictured her, myself, coming into my office. I greet her, motion and we sit on the beige upholstered chairs with wooden arms, facing each other. There she is in front of me, a slim pale woman with black hair falling in waves to her shoulders, distracted eyes, her gaze landing somewhere to my right. "Becky," I say, and I hear something familiar in my voice, an ease, a warmth which even in that first spoken word holds out not the promise but the possibility of acceptance, of being held. "Can you explain to me what has brought you here?"

The next morning I went to my desk, took out a blank notebook, and started to write. It mattered to me to do this by hand, I didn't know why.

October 17

BECKY THERAPIST: Good morning, Becky.

BECKY CLIENT: Morning.

BECKY THERAPIST: I'm glad to see you....can you tell me what brings you here?

BECKY CLIENT: I'm pregnant. I don't know what to do.

BECKY THERAPIST: What to do...

BECKY CLIENT: Whether to, you know....I can't say it.

BECKY THERAPIST: So there's a decision you need to make and it's so hard you can't even say what it is.

BECKY CLIENT: Yes.

BECKY THERAPIST: Can you tell me how you got pregnant?

BECKY CLIENT: The usual way....okay, I know what you're asking. I was having sex with this guy and something happened with the condom.

BECKY THERAPIST: Something happened?

BECKY CLIENT: I don't...remember. Exactly what happened with the condom, I don't know. Maybe it broke. Maybe he never put it on. We'd had a lot to drink. I had a lot to drink. I...I fucked up.

BECKY THERAPIST: So you and the man had a lot to drink, and something went wrong with the condom but you can't remember what. And you feel it was your fault. Is that right?

BECKY CLIENT: Yes.

BECKY THERAPIST: Can you tell me about the man?

BECKY CLIENT: There's nothing to tell.

BECKY THERAPIST: Because?

BECKY CLIENT: Just a guy I dated for a couple of months. A fucking prick.

BECKY THERAPIST: It sounds like you're mad at him?

BECKY CLIENT: I'm mad at myself.

BECKY THERAPIST: You're mad at yourself for fucking up?

BECKY CLIENT: Yes.

BECKY THERAPIST: For dating a man you didn't respect?

BECKY CLIENT: For dating him and getting drunk with him and having sex without a fucking condom and look at what I've gone and done to myself.

BECKY THERAPIST: So to you this pregnancy is something you've done to yourself.

BECKY CLIENT: Yes.

BECKY THERAPIST: Are there other things you're feeling? About being pregnant?

BECKY CLIENT: I feel...I don't know what I feel....Okay, I know what I don't feel. I don't feel like I know how to be a mother. I don't feel like I can take this child's life. I don't feel like this is really happening....I feel confused....Not completely confused. I feel scared. I feel like a piece of shit.

October 18

BECKY THERAPIST: Can you tell me about your family?

BECKY CLIENT: My family? What's that got to do with anything?

BT: Well...

BC: Right, you think something bad happened to me when I was little, I'm scarred by all the shit my mother did wrong and now I'm scared I'll turn out to be the same kind of mother she is. Tell me something I don't already fucking know.

BT: So you're aware of how you've been affected by your mother, and it sounds like you want me to be respectful of what you already know about yourself.

BC: I want you not to be asking me those stock questions therapists always ask.

BT: It's really important for me to see you as your own person, not as a generic client who I would ask the same questions I ask everyone like I'm ticking down a prepared list. Is that right?

BC: Well yeah.

BT: Is there more you'd like to say about what you expect from me?

BC: What I expect from you? I'm not even sure what you're talking about. I mean look, I don't come here with a list of prepared questions for you.

BT: Why do you come here? Do you know? Is it something you can say?

BC: I came here because I wanted you to fucking solve my problem.

BT: You want me to help you decide whether to keep the child.

BC: I don't want you to help me decide! I want you to fucking tell me what to do! You're supposed to be the wise woman around here.

BT: *You're looking for wisdom from me that you feel you don't...*

BC: *You're not going to tell me. Are you.*

BT: *No.*

BC: *Then what good are you?*

BT: *You feel so alone with this.*

BC: *No shit.*

BT: *I can be here with you.*

BC: *That's it? That's all I get from the great and mighty therapist in the sky?*

BT: *For now, yes.*

Near the end of the morning on Sunday I started feeling nauseous. Finally a physical response to being pregnant? Or an emotional response? Or just some random stomach bug?

Whatever the cause, it gave me a reason to cancel with my mother, for which I was grateful even if I had to endure her shit on the phone.

"Rebecca what do you mean, you're not coming to dinner? I bought a whole chicken just for this."

"I'm sure you and Dad will manage to eat the chicken, Mom. Or you can freeze it for next time."

"What are you talking about, freeze the chicken? I do not *freeze* chicken. You expect me to serve thawed frozen chicken in my house?"

I have already reached the point in the conversation where I start wondering what life would be like with a mother—I always want to say a normal mother, but I've seen too many versions of normal to believe the word has any value, it's just a way of saying a mother who would have been attuned to my needs. I stretch out on my bed and rub my distressed tummy and say, "Fine, Mom, then cook the chicken. Why does this have to be such a big deal?"

It's the wrong question to ask, I know this as the words are coming out of my mouth, and now my mother is off to the races, bemoaning that I just don't care, no one cares and no one has any understanding of what she goes through and it has always been like this and why should she think it would ever change. Her voice raises toward the same crescendo I have heard a thousand times and I know when it will crack, when the tears will start. These are parts in a script we keep playing out, I know all of it so well except for the one thing that would matter, which is how to change the script.

October 21

BECKY CLIENT: Okay, let's talk about my fucking family. Three days since that lovely phone call with my mother and I can't get her out of my head. The woman drives me CRAZY. I call and say I'm not feeling well and does she once even have the itsy bitsy decency to show the slightest bit of concern about me? What a fucking stupid question, of course it's all about her, it's me having the gall to make her life miserable by being sick to my stomach, and would it occur to her that just maybe someone who is sick to her stomach might possibly not be the ideal dinner guest? Another stupid question and it's not like there is any new information here. She taught me a long time ago whose needs matter and everything here is old, there is only history condemned to repeat itself and the real question, the one I actually don't know the answer to is why she gets me every single fucking time. I'm like a fly who keeps getting caught in the same web and manages to squirm free and then flies straight back into the exact same web again and presumably, I mean you would think that I have a slightly larger brain than a fly but there is no learning curve here at all, brain size is apparently beside the point and something else is going on that is completely beyond my grasp.

BECKY THERAPIST: So when you told your mother on Sunday that you were sick to your stomach and not coming to dinner, her entire response was about how this was affecting her and she didn't show the slightest bit of concern about you. It sounds like you feel so deeply hurt and out of control—you know this is what your mother is like, but you're not able to make any use of your knowledge, you're like a fly that keeps getting caught in the same trap. Is that right?

BC: Yeah. It's right. Really, what good is this supposed to do? I tell you what I already know, and it doesn't do anything for me. You tell me what I already know, and somehow that is supposed to do something for me?

BT: You feel hopeless about your relationship with your mother.

BC: Yes!

BT: And it sounds like you blame yourself...

BC: Yes! I'm an idiot.

BT: Do you want to talk about how your relationship with your mother, your hopelessness and not being able to break out of the pattern, how this affects...

BC:...my great decision in the sky? I already told you I'm scared I'll end up being like her.

BT: Do you have other feelings about your mother?

BC: Other feelings? Look, since I was eight years old I have been trying to not be like her. I would say there has been nothing more important in my life. And after thirty fucking years I still feel like I can't get out from under her.

BT: What happened when you were eight?

BC: When I was eight...okay, I'll tell you. This may sound stupid.....It was just a regular day after school and I was helping my mother with dinner like I always did, she called me her wonderful little helper. I had already peeled the potatoes and cut them up and put them in the pot to boil, and I had set the table and I thought I was done but then she told me to slice tomatoes and cucumbers for the salad and I said no. I never said no when she told me to do something. I liked being her helper and I liked it when she smiled and said nice things about me, but this one time I did say no and here's why. That day in school a girl named Alice made friends with me. Out on the playground she asked me to jump rope together and then we talked and giggled and found out we had stuff in common, and we traded phone numbers and I really wanted to go call her before dinner and that's the reason I said no to my mother. I said no and she slapped me. That never happened in our house, neither of my parents ever hit me but that day it did happen and I didn't understand what was going on, it was that fast. She didn't even hit me that hard but that wasn't the point. The point is this is what happens when you say no to your mother, and then it was like behind the slap was her face, and her face was even worse than the slap. I stood there frozen and I looked up at her and I could see in her eyes the way she was glaring down at me and her lips were like trembling *or something, and there was just this hatred for me, all because I said no to her, all because I wouldn't slice some stupid fucking tomatoes and cucumbers....okay, I know lots of kids get slapped by their parents and it only happened to me once and it sounds like just some stupid little incident that I should have gotten over, and well it was stupid, but it wasn't little and I didn't get over it. She always said how much she loved me and how great I was and adorable and precious and you name it, and before that I believed her, I mean why wouldn't I, but that day I found out that nothing was the way it had seemed, and nothing ever would be that way between my mother and me. I didn't even have words for it, but I knew.*

BT: It sounds like for the first time you saw your mother as she really was, and your world crumbled.

BC: Yeah, and for the first time I saw myself for who I really am.

BT: Which is?

BC: Which is a fucking idiot.

BT: Because?

BC: Because I let her trick me for all those years.

In the space of a few days steady dull nausea had become my background noise. I was still no closer to any kind of decision.

It occurred to me that there was another option, I could have the baby and put her up for adoption, I know this seems obvious but for five and a half weeks it honestly hadn't crossed my mind, and at first it seemed like the solution to my dilemma, the prescribed way to not take a life and not be a mother. But then I let myself remember what this option actually meant. I would be abandoning my baby. I would bring a child into the world to be traumatized at birth, the immediate overwhelming blows of separation and loss, a grief of inconceivable proportions for a newborn. Yes there are wonderful adoptive families, yes there are adopted kids who live good lives, I knew these things but I also knew that I did not want to do this to a child born from my body.

Four

After Lathsamy passed the bar she started working as a care and protection attorney, earning a fraction of what she could have made coming out of Harvard if she had gone into corporate law. She represented children whose parents were being charged by the state with abuse or neglect. It was an aspect of her recovery, this work she chose, a way for her to have some impact on the mistreatment of children in the world. I don't think she was under any illusions about how much she or any one person could accomplish, and while she identified with her clients she certainly didn't believe her work in the present could undo what had been done to her in the past. It was more that she wanted to use her own experience for the good of others, to do for them what had not been done for her. Devoting herself to vulnerable children was a way of healing and she would talk about the Buddhist concept of turning poison into medicine; that was what she saw herself doing.

Through her work she met Jeffrey, a social worker who investigated allegations of abuse and neglect. They had common clients, common interests, became friends and then began a delicate progression of steps toward intimacy. He was the first man she had gone out with since her breakdown in law school, and of course she had many fears, of attachment, of sex, of revealing her true self. She recounted to me how when she told him the story of her childhood there was no flinching, no pity, he held her with his eyes and it was as if in some way he already knew, not the particulars but the self beneath the particulars. He had understood she was the survivor of atrocities, and hearing them spoken was only confirming a connection that already had been made. Jeffrey told Lathsamy about his own history of being bullied by older brothers and by boys at school, of not having been protected by parents and teachers, and while these were hardly atrocities, he knew trauma from the inside, and that—along with a sensibility to the human condition, an emotional openness that had somehow withstood the long years of male conditioning—made it possible for him to embrace her as an equal.

He waited for her to be ready for sex, told her that nothing was more important to him than for this to be her choice, the expression of her undivided willingness and desire. After Lathsamy made the choice she told me, "He was gentle with me, Becky. In bed. I never knew a man could be so gentle." She blinked and smiled and tears ran down her cheeks.

It became an antidote, this relationship, to the sexual encounter she'd had in law school which had unleashed her memories, to previous experiences with men in the States as an adolescent and young adult. Nothing could be an antidote to what had happened in Bangkok, but Jeffrey embodied for her the other end of the human continuum, that goodness existed in the world, that connection was possible, that these possibilities still lived in her.

I thought of what Lathsamy had said in the past about hope, how far she had come from that place where hope had held no meaning for her. Now here she was, opening to the tenderness of another person, allowing herself to be touched, able to love and be loved. Something huge had shifted, she called it the changing of her karma, and witnessing this I could feel a wave crest and stream inside me, a physical sensation, my own flowing amazement.

Their wedding was a Buddhist ceremony, a hundred people chanted *nam-myoho-renge-kyo,* and during the vows Jeffrey told Lathsamy that he would keep his heart open to her for as long as he lived. Then

Lathsamy read a poem she had written called "Three Thousand Possibilities." The title referred to a belief in Nicheren Buddhism, which Lathsamy had explained to me, that there are ten life conditions, what the Buddhists call worlds, ranging from Hell and Bestiality to the enlightened states of the Bodhisattva and the Buddha, and each life condition contains within it the possibility of all the other worlds. Somehow this adds up to three thousand possibilities in each moment of life, and while I couldn't quite follow the math, I understood how profound it was for Lathsamy, this way of understanding human experience. This is what she read:

The present.
What does it mean, this moment?

A flower blooms
Speck in the vastness.
Time and space.
The flower is you
Your vast heart
Here, now.

And I? And we?
I bloom.
We bloom.
The flower is us.

We.
Against all odds.

One in three thousand.

I sat there and cried, was aware of others crying, and this was not the ordinary sentimentality of a wedding, it was a celebration of Lathsamy as a person, the distance she had traveled, really something inexpressible, the suffering she carried and this place of joy she had come to.

In the first year of their marriage they decided to have a child. Lathsamy feared that something had been broken in her which would make this impossible, but in fact she conceived easily and had a normal pregnancy. For her it was a statement of such remarkable determination and hope, this choice to become a mother. At many sessions over the course of her pregnancy she talked to me about what it meant to her, raising a child to live with an unshakable foundation of safety and acceptance and love, things that sound so ordinary from the mouth of an expecting mother but which for her were the ultimate embodiment of turning poison into medicine.

Trying for a natural childbirth, she was in labor for fifty hours before finally giving birth by C-section to Edward Bounmy, a healthy eight pound baby boy.

After the birth Lathsamy went into a postpartum depression. The exhaustion from her long labor didn't ease. She felt the C-section was her failure. She struggled with breast feeding; when Eddie clamped his gums down on her nipple she said she felt assaulted, the last thing she wanted to be feeling. The harder she tried to relax, to immerse herself in love for her child, the tenser she became. The baby must have picked up on her tension, creating a vicious circle. When she managed to nurse, she felt he was sucking the life out of her. With encouragement from Jeffrey she switched to formula, another failure in her mind and heart. She blamed Jeffrey, feeling that he had led her to give up on breast feeding too soon. Jeffrey was undoubtedly experiencing his own stresses, a new baby and a depressed wife who was rapidly pulling away from him and the child. Lathsamy complained about Jeffrey becoming irritable, which she felt was her fault but it made her angrier anyway, one more thing she didn't want to feel and couldn't help, and she pulled away even more. She felt trapped, her needs so abruptly out of sync with those of her son and her husband, leaving her light years removed from everything about parenthood she had envisioned, not understanding how this could be happening, not knowing what to do.

Jeffrey had to go back to work. Left alone with the baby, Lathsamy panicked. She began cutting herself again, something she hadn't done in almost five years. When Eddie was napping she would go into the bathroom and use a razor blade on the tops of her forearms and thighs, careful to avoid veins, etching long thin trails of red. She told me it was the only thing that gave her any relief, the only way she could get through the long days. She was afraid that if she didn't injure herself she would harm the baby. She didn't tell Jeffrey, made sure he didn't see her body, felt endless shame, felt sure she was harming the baby emotionally if not physically just by being who she was.

I referred Lathsamy to a psychiatrist, a decent woman who prescribed an anti-depressant which helped but not very much. I referred her to a group for new mothers struggling with depression; she was too depressed and ashamed to go. I asked if she was writing about her depression, the kinds of short pieces she had shown me before, or poems, or anything. She said she wasn't. I suggested she try. Lathsamy looked at me as if I had said something impossible; her face went tight and hard and she answered in an injured voice, "Becky when would I find the time to write? Where would I find the energy? Don't you understand? I can barely get out of bed." My first thought was to say, You find the time and energy to get out of bed and cut yourself in the bathroom, but I didn't. Instead I reminded myself to listen to what she was telling me and see this from her point of view, help her to feel heard and respected, avoid the trap of getting into a fight that we would both lose.

I encouraged her to resume her Buddhist practice and that she did, chanting twice a day and returning to her study group. This helped, she said, more than anything. She seemed to level out, still depressed but managing to attend to the baby, not able to go back to work but having regained some connection with Jeffrey. Functioning took all her energy, she slept whenever the baby slept, and much of the time she worried about not being the mother she'd imagined; but she struggled with her characteristic courage to be the best mother she could.

Six months later, for no apparent reason, she plummeted again. She talked to me about looking at Eddie and feeling that life was something she had inflicted on him. She told the psychiatrist, who was aware of her cutting, that she felt like slitting her wrists. Lathsamy was hospitalized. Tests done as part of a routine medical screening found that her blood sugar was 550, more than 400 points above normal, and her thyroid hormone was dangerously low. Diabetes and hypothyroidism are both conditions that can affect depression. Ten days later she came out of the hospital on insulin injections, oral diabetes and thyroid medications, a different antidepressant, and pills for anxiety.

The hospital discharge summary, sent to me with Lathsamy's permission, described her as a thirty-three year old Asian woman who looked older than her age. I realized this was true and that I had missed it, how much the ordeal of the last several months had aged her. I had focused on the toll parenthood was taking on her emotionally but not physically. The physical changes must have happened gradually and when you see someone every week you can overlook this kind of thing, miss its magnitude, but nevertheless what I had allowed myself not to see, or to see but not to name, and by not naming not fully take in, was jarring. I had always thought of Lathsamy as looking youthful. Even in those early days when she was twenty-eight and came to me after her first hospitalization, maybe especially then, she had the aspect of an abandoned, terrified little girl. Later I watched her grow into a vibrant, determined young woman with flashing eyes. During most of her pregnancy she glowed. Now she stepped into my office with a slow forced gait, her eyes downcast, and I realized that what made her look older than her years, more than the circles under her eyes or the other lines of fatigue and stress, was her air of defeat, something that even in her most desperate moments I had never seen before.

Bessel van der Kolk, a psychiatrist and leading figure in the treatment of trauma, has written about the biochemistry of traumatic stress.

He calls it the body keeping score. The gist is that the body stores trauma in the brain and throughout the central nervous system. There are actual neuronal changes that can last for years and years and wreak all kinds of havoc, psychological and physical. Memories get blocked and then released. Pain gets numbed and then roars to life. The most primitive parts of the brain are destabilized and either shut down or go into overdrive. And van der Kolk cites research showing that sexually abused girls are more likely to have endocrine diseases like diabetes and hypothyroidism.

The body keeps score. But all those things we had told ourselves, Lathsamy and I, about the strength and vitality of her recovery—were they so much fluff? Some variation on the house-of-cards achievements of her adolescence and early adulthood, constructed on denial? I still didn't think so, but there she was, this woman suddenly older than her years, and her healthy thriving self was up against forces lodged inside her body that could only be kept at bay for so long.

* * *

Lathsamy came home from the hospital and rallied once again. Having her blood sugar and thyroid regulated helped in many ways, not least that these newly diagnosed illnesses were something tangible to focus on, an explanation for her recent acute depression, ways to perform self-care, in the case of the insulin injections several times a day. She told me she found it soothing to test her blood sugar and give herself shots. It offered her a respite from the demands of her baby, her marriage. It also rearranged, one more time, her self, now into someone with identified illnesses, perhaps creating more space for her own needs. That, or something less rational, helped her to maintain some sort of equilibrium.

She was able to function as a mother, reported having tender feelings for Jeffrey, having regained enough perspective to see and appreciate how difficult her depression was for him and how hard he was trying. A little after Eddie's first birthday Lathsamy went back to work part time, and though at first she said she barely had the stamina for it, working was also a reclaiming of one of the good things from her life before childbirth, a realm of uncomplicated competence. Of course it also gave her a break from parenting. Over time her stamina increased, and working seemed to help her to be a little more comfortable as a mother, more affectionate as a spouse.

Still there was a tenuousness. In her face, her voice, the way she carried herself, things she told me of her doubts and fears, and her accounts of how every day was a struggle. She continued to find private moments to self-injure. Her sense of defeat seemed to have morphed into a kind of resignation, a heaviness that clinically you might call an underlying depression. Or a prolonged grieving. Or was it, more hopefully, a maturing acceptance of her limitations?

Oh, have I mentioned how fucking sick I am of hearing about Latsemy or whatever her stupid name is? Why should *she* get all the attention? Okay, some bad things happened to her but what about me? What about all the shit that happened to me? Does the Fucking Bitch tell my story? Does she go on and on about how I did this and I did that, how courageous I am and how tragic my life has been?

No, of course she doesn't. Instead she locked me up in this fucking dungeon and spends her time pretending to care and showering it on What's Her Name. That's the FB for you.

About now you're probably thinking that all I do is whine and feel sorry for myself. Well who else do I have to feel sorry for me? Besides, that isn't all I do. I hate her fucking guts, that's something else. And here's one more thing—I tell the truth. Who else do you see around here doing that?

You??...I act as though there's someone out there I'm talking to, someone who could possibly listen to me, let alone give a flying fuck. What a joke, who do I think I'm kidding?

Five

Another Friday, the conclusion of Week Six, and nothing was concluded.

I had not filled Lathsamy's slot at the end of Friday afternoon, not for lack of referrals but because I didn't feel I could. For six months it had been an empty space in my day, in my life, the only thing that seemed fitting. Ten years of work, the kind of bond that transcends whatever it means to call someone a client, and now this. I walked home with dusk approaching, the day gray and dreary, unseasonably warm, the leaves dulled, the air moist and oppressive, the weekend blank, nothing right.

October 25

BECKY THERAPIST: What about the rest of your family?
BECKY CLIENT: The rest of my family? Are you serious? Look, I'm in a desperate situation, I have one fucking week left to abort with pills and I am getting nowhere and you want me to sit here and talk about my father and my brother? As if they have anything to do with this. I mean sure I idealized my father when I was growing up, sure he falls short of the person I thought he was, sure he has a problem with

alcohol, yes he has affairs even at his age, and believe me if you had been married to my mother for the last forty-six years you would drink too much and you would have affairs, and the point is that absolutely none of this has the slightest thing to do with why I can't decide whether to keep this child. And yes my brother and I inhabit different planets, Mark Hoffman the hotshot attorney who works for Exxon-Mobil and lives in some ritzy Virginia suburb of DC with the perfect wife and the perfect little girls and it's true that I think his values suck and I'm sure he would think the same about me if he ever even thought about me or my values, and yes when we were kids we had nothing to do with each other and yes I was the pesky little sister whose existence he barely acknowledged, and yes he left for college when I was ten and I grew up feeling like an only child but really so what? And now you're going to tell me I sound angry and isn't that something we should explore when what I'm angry about is that I have seven days left to make a decision, less than seven days because if I'm going to use pills I have to make the appointment first and get the prescription and that takes time, I'm running out of time and I am not getting any help here.

BT: So you're feeling desperate because you're running out of time to decide whether to abort with pills, and you're not making any progress toward deciding, and you're angry because I'm asking about things that don't have any bearing on your decision.

BC: Well—yeah. Right.

BT: And the decision feels impossible because they are both things, aborting and having the child, you feel so strongly that neither of them are tenable options.

BC: Tenable options. Such pristine clinical language.

BT: So my language feels cold and removed, when for you this is something you are so much right in the middle of, this excruciating thing of having both choices feel so impossible.

BC: That's a little better....okay, look. I know I'm giving you a hard time, I know this isn't your fault, I know that what I want from you, for you to make this decision for me, I know that isn't possible either, I know I'm angry about this whole mess and I'm taking it out on you and it isn't fair. But I have to have someone to be angry at!

BT: It's fine for you to be angry at me.

BC: No it isn't. That can't be true.

BT: It's fine with me. Actually more than fine, it's great for you to be expressing your feelings.

BC: Okay, if you say so but it isn't really getting us anywhere, is it? I mean here I am, mouthing off and acting like a petulant little girl and if you're good with that, well, great but how is that helping me make this decision?

At the end of Week Seven I was giddy with relief and panic. Still no decision, which meant that pills were out and I had a full two months to decide whether to abort by aspiration. It seemed like a reprieve, a glorious expanse of time to sit with my indecision, to struggle and somehow find the alchemy which would turn it into a choice, and at the same time I felt a gnawing certainty that I was incapable of choosing, that I was deciding by not deciding, and rather than me making this impossible decision, the decision was going to make me, or unmake me. In my mind I had been treating this—the end of the window in which pills were possible—I had believed it was a real deadline. I had told myself that aspiration was too brutal to consider. Now the supposed deadline had passed and I was nowhere, I was stepping into a new version of reality in which aspiration was very much something to consider and I had in no way committed myself to having the child and there was a new deadline, and why would that be any different from the first one? What was going on in my mind seemed to have little to do with what was going on in my heart, in my mildly nauseous belly, whatever place inside me was driving this failure to decide.

I found myself thinking that I should talk to someone. As long as I had been convinced that the time was short and I could force a resolution, a hope which was being contradicted every day by my inability to resolve anything—but these things are not rational—I managed to justify keeping this to myself because there was an end-date fast approaching, whatever sense that did or didn't make. Now I told myself that two more months of being alone with this, a self-imposed isolation, was not smart, not necessary. Yes, I had my journal and it was good, but at the end of the day it was an imaginary conversation, not the same as talking to a real person outside of myself.

I thought of telling my father. I wanted to but I just knew that if I told him it would only be a matter to time before my mother found out; he would let it slip when he'd been drinking or he would feel guilty about keeping it from her, and even the slightest chance of my mother getting hold of this made me frantic. Besides I didn't feel it was fair to ask my father to keep a secret.

The obvious person was my best friend, Hannah, and I decided to tell her, at least I thought I would. We've known each other since graduate school, we're in a supervision group together, we have always been able to talk about personal issues, boyfriends, her marital problems, my mother. I went out with her for dinner at an Indian restaurant in Central Square, a favorite spot for both of us, and I kept waiting for the right moment which kept not coming. Hannah was fretting about her appearance, how much weight she had gained since she got married, twenty-five pounds and counting; she had been slim and blond and now look at her, and she and her husband had been fighting, sex was not great and she couldn't help believing he wasn't attracted to her anymore, and wasn't it only a matter of time before he started having affairs? Hannah is not a superficial or unaware person, she knows that a good marriage is built on more than physical attraction and there were things going on that had nothing to do with her weight. But she also knew how men were and in particular she knew her husband, and she didn't feel she could act as though twenty-five pounds was something to be ignored. Besides there was the underlying thing of feeling out of control of her body and what she was putting into it, and here it was happening right as we spoke, the *samosas* and the *korma* dish she'd ordered with all that cream, hardly a dinner for losing weight.

I sat there listening, nodding, empathizing, asking questions, offering suggestions, the things a friend is supposed to do, and it was genuine in its own way but at the same time I felt a hundred miles away from her. Behind Hannah there was a glass wall with a full view of the restaurant's kitchen; men moved gracefully in their white jackets, flames quivered under skillets and pans and it was all I could do to keep my attention from being drawn away from Hannah and into the activity on the other side of the glass. I found myself thinking that her problems paled compared to mine, and the next instant I thought *I hate you*, my stomach was suddenly in an uproar, I could feel the edge of my dinner rising into my throat and I wanted to yell at her, the words were perched on my tongue, *Listen to me Hannah! I am fucking pregnant and I'm overwhelmed and I could use a little attention here and all you can do is talk about your own pathetic self!* It took every ounce of control not to say it, to push the food back down, still whatever it was that was racing through my arms, my legs, pounding my head. I told myself I was being absurdly unfair, that Hannah was only being herself and this was my shit, I had to own it, none of it was her fault. Then I wondered if Hannah had picked up on the outburst that had just erupted an inch below my surface. If she did she showed no sign of it, which made me feel that much further removed from her.

I tried to talk myself back to where I'd started—I could still tell Hannah I was pregnant, the entire point of the evening. I knew one of the issues between Hannah and her husband was when to have a child. Her clock was ticking and now with the drama that was mounting in their marriage they might be drifting into a question of whether rather than when. I kept waiting for her to bring this up, thinking it could be the perfect segue, and she never did.

Finally our waiter, a young brown skinned man with jet black hair and a thick Indian accent, stopped at our table to see if we wanted dessert. Hannah shot me a look that asked how much pain she was going to inflict on herself in one evening. It took her a long minute to say no thanks. The waiter wandered off and Hannah said what a comfort it was to be able to talk to me. She got teary, apologized for taking up so much space in the conversation, then asked what was going on with me. I heard myself complain about my mother, ask why I kept letting myself get sucked into her craziness, and everything I said was true but I felt like I was playacting, hiding behind my routine script. Why? I had no clue, I just couldn't say the words I'm pregnant and I don't think I ever felt so false with a friend, so far away, trapped inside my own skin.

November 2

BECKY CLIENT: Okay no questions from you today; if anyone is asking questions it's going to be me and as a matter of fact I do have a question: what exactly is the matter with me? I almost went off on Hannah, I mean what the fuck?

Here's another one. Could it be that the only reason I don't want to be a mother is that I'm scared, okay terrified, I'll be like my mother? The answer is no, that could not possibly be the only reason for all this drama. What is it I don't know about myself? I can't even think where to start. You would say to start with my feelings, but I don't know what—all right, terror. Not just terrified of being like my mother, but plain terrified. It doesn't make any sense, but there it is. I really do feel like something's wrong with me, I mean it would be one thing to say, I choose not to be a mother, I as a woman choose not to follow the scripted life, and anyway it's the twenty-first fucking century and how long does the script have to hound us, and lots of women choose not to be mothers, have been choosing not to be mothers for years and years. How hard really should it be for me to say look, I'm thirty-eight years old and I have a career, work that I love and a life that doesn't happen to include being saddled with raising a child; single mother or not it's just something that doesn't call to me. It wouldn't be hard at all if that's where I were at, but the point is that's not where I'm at. This isn't about my career, it isn't about my identity as a woman, I don't fucking know what it's about and that is the point.

BECKY THERAPIST: You're realizing that your terror of being like your mother is not the only reason why it feels impossible to you to have the child, there is something else going on that you're missing, something deep that you don't know about yourself. Your terror also goes beyond your identity as a woman and the feminine script, and it makes you feel like something is wrong with you.

BECKY CLIENT: Right, yeah. Or look at it another way and I could say, fine I made a massive mistake and here I am pregnant and now I need to take responsibility for it, and my mistake is not the fault of this life that's forming in me and I just don't feel capable of taking that life, so I will live with the consequences of my mistake and have this child. Logical, straightforward, commendable, the right thing to do and a bunch of shit.

BT: So whatever is happening in you, the forces that are actually driving you don't relate at all to the idea of taking responsibility for a mistake.

BC: Right, whatever. Tell me, what the fuck is the point of this? I know I keep saying that but isn't it just possible there is no actual point? Let's be real, I'm talking myself in circles and you're the goddess of hearing what I say and as far as I can tell that's the only thing you do. Fine, I'm being heard. So what?

BT: It sounds like you're feeling so hopeless.
BC: Yes I feel fucking hopeless!

Before dinner on Sunday my dad had the decency to ask if I wanted a drink instead of just handing me a glass of wine, and when I said no thanks, he nodded and poured his own and asked me what was new, taking me in stride the way he always has. By the time my mother called us to the table he was on his third glass; even if I hadn't seen him drink the first two I would have known by the animation in his face, the puns I have never found especially amusing, but I take him in stride too.

Between the living room and kitchen is our dining room with its long wooden table which as far as I know my mother has only ever used once a year at Thanksgiving. From the dining room there's a doorway to the large kitchen. In between the refrigerator on the left, the stove to the right and the double sink straight ahead with counters on both sides and cupboards above and below there is a lot of open space; you could do something with it like put up an island but my mother would never consider such a thing. On the far side of the stove a little hall leads to the back door. Past the fridge, walls extend to mark an entryway to an adjoining space that Mom has always called the breakfast room, a name that never made any sense to me because that's where we had all our meals when I was growing up. It has a table big enough to seat four which as long as I can remember has been covered with the same vinyl tablecloth, its plain blue interspersed with tacky images of flowers in orange, green and pink, and I know that one tablecloth can only last for so long, but when one wears out my mother must replace it with the identical pattern.

The table is next to a window that in daylight looks out onto the backyard with its cherry tree that blossomed like clockwork on the first of May, filling the yard with white petals which I would stare at while suffering through meals and trying to ignore my mother. We have our assigned seats, Mom at the end toward the kitchen so she can bring food to the table and then sit and get up in the middle of a meal if something is needed, Dad and I across from each other which allows for the most subtle possible knowing glances. Sitting down with them to a meal always makes me feel like I never left, like I'm still the kid who's bracing for one more installment of a struggle she always manages to lose.

As we made our way to the table my father was talking to me about a New York State sex abuse case. A twenty-six year old woman in a town near Rochester walked out of a supermarket and crossed paths with an older man who smiled at her; something about him struck her as familiar and suddenly she remembered being dragged into an alley and raped when she was a girl and this was the man who did it. The case made the media because the man actually admitted committing the rape, then retracted, and he couldn't be prosecuted under the New York statute of limitations which had run out when the woman turned twenty-three.

We reached the table and my mother was carefully placing a platter full of roast chicken in the middle. My attention was drawn in more directions than I could count, my father chattering on about the Rochester woman and the archaic New York law, how much more enlightened we were in Massachusetts, what did I think, and naturally I thought it was terrible; the chicken on the platter and whether Mom after all had frozen the one from when I was sick, a question I didn't dare ask; the sight of my mother, shrunken and stooped, her movements stiff and labored, her short straight hair dyed brown to mask her age, and I found myself wondering how much older she would look if she let her hair go white; and finally, something else, stirring inside my body, a kind of deep emotional rumbling that there was no way I could do anything but ignore.

My father was going off on a tangent about Freud's view of sexual trauma and my mother said, "Sam!" Her voice was sharp, aggrieved, frantic—and all she had to do was say my father's name in that way for me to know exactly what she wanted.

"What is it, Leah," my father said, annoyed, raising his palms.

"This is my time with Rebecca."

Rebecca, I was not going to react and there was no chance anyway because my parents were busy sniping at each other.

"What are you talking about, your time? We're sitting here at the table together."

"You had all that time with her in the living room while I was making the meal and you don't lift a goddamn finger to help, and now she's in here and it's my turn, Sam."

I caught my father's eye and we had been through this often enough for him to get that I was pleading with him to let it go. I saw his face contort, like a man bracing to lift a weight, then it went slack, his shoulders sagged and he reached for his wine.

My mother waited for my father to say something and when he didn't she turned to me and said, "Rebecca, I see you're not having a glass of wine with your dinner?" Her voice was completely different, all the venom gone as if she had turned a valve to stop the flow.

"No."

"You didn't the last time, either. It's quite a change. I take it you've stopped drinking?"

There was no point in trying to dance around her question, so I just said a quiet "Yes" and hoped she would drop it, but of course she didn't.

"What is it, something with your health?"

This might have sounded like concern, especially pieced together with my having canceled the last time supposedly because of my health, but I knew better. My mother stopped drinking in her early sixties when she was diagnosed with a stomach ulcer and her doctor advised that alcohol would cause her agony. If that was why she quit, then it must be something similar for me; I know her and that is how she thinks. I also know how much deeper it goes than thinking, it is embedded in her psyche, in the entire way she experiences the world: she carries this conviction that she and I are the same person. No amount of evidence to the contrary, say for example that she stopped drinking in her sixties and I'm thirty-eight, or that she married at twenty-five and I'm still single, or that she worked in real estate and I'm a therapist, or that I have reacted against her in every way I could, none of these inconvenient realities can shake her underlying conviction. If I insist on failing to be the self she has mapped out for me, the person who is her own self mirrored back to her, it's only some perverse thing I do to make her suffer.

"No Mom," I said. "It's not because of my health."

"Then why?"

My father, his glass already empty again, winced and said, "Leah, she doesn't have to have a reason, why don't you... ."

"Why don't you just stay out of this, Sam," my mother snapped back. "I'm trying to have a conversation with my daughter. Of course she has a reason." She glared at him; my body tensed, one more moment when she was pushing him to the edge of a cliff they had been jumping off together all my life. My father looked down, made a noise with his shoe on the floor, picked up his fork and snared a piece of chicken, let it hang in the air and finally put it in his mouth. "Tell me Rebecca," my mother said, her voice still harsh, not able now to shut off her resentment at my father's interference, her annoyance at my terse inadequate answers, "why have you decided to stop drinking?"

I hated the way she was cross-examining me, I wanted to tell her to fuck off and of course there was no way that I could. "No particular reason, Mom. I've just reached a point in my life where I don't want to drink."

"All right, I can see that you're not going to tell me, so that will just have to be how it is."

She pouted and neither of us dared to say a word, my father and I, not under the pall my mother cast over the table. The pall lifted by slow degrees, I know her pouts so well and how they subside. Sitting next to her I could feel her emotions pulsating like a live wire. She picked at her food, sipped her water, took in a breath and let it out, collected herself and said, "Your brother and Christine and the girls will be coming for Thanksgiving."

It was hardly a surprise, my brother and his family always come for Thanksgiving, the one time a year I see them. But I thought she was making an effort to find something neutral to talk about. "They're staying here, I assume?"

"Yes, of course and I'll make the meal."

"It isn't too much?"

"What are you talking about, too much?" She dismissed the thought with a wave of her hand. "Who else is going to make the meal?"

"I can help..."

"Don't be silly." I knew she wouldn't let me help, honestly I don't even know why I bothered saying it. "Is there anyone you'd like to bring?"

It was thinly veiled code, her question. "No, Mom."

"I thought there was someone you were seeing?"

"We broke up."

"When was this?"

"A couple of months ago, Mom."

"And you don't tell me?"

So much for the neutral topic, so much for the lull in the cross-examination. I could feel myself bristle and at the same time the words *I'm sorry* reflexively started to form, and I stopped them before they got out. I was not going to apologize to her for having my own life, and without missing a beat she filled the silence.

"Rebecca, listen to me. You're thirty-eight years old and you are not getting any younger. It's time you got serious about your life. You have these whatever you call them, relationships, affairs, flings, you see a man for a few months, I can't even keep track. It's time for you to find yourself a nice man and get married and start a family. By the time I was your age I was thirteen years married already, with two children and a house in Newton, this very house. Tell me, what are you waiting for?"

"For Christ sake, Leah!" My father's voice and I didn't sense it coming. I have been focusing on my mother, trying to let myself feel the bottomless hurt in her eyes, the lifetime of stress, the yearning unmet need etched into the lines of her face, trying and failing to pretend that she is my client (an old trick that never works), trying and failing to feel sorry for her instead of angry, trying and failing to feel anger instead of rage, trying so hard to keep my rage from erupting, and instead the outburst comes from my father. "Leave the girl alone, will you? Yes, she's thirty-eight years old. Can't you just once in your life let her be?"

My mother snarls back at him and there they go over the cliff; the whole dinner has been building to this moment when the alcohol finally releases my father's tongue, when my mother gets to vent fifty years of grievances, when their voices become machetes and I sit here small and quiet, the story of my fucking life.

Explain one thing to me, how can an adult woman be so fucking clueless? After all this time I still don't get it. Statute of limitations? I'm not even sure what that means and I understand it better than her. Which isn't saying much, because I could count on the fingers of one hand all the things she does understand and still have a bunch of fingers to spare. Okay, she understands stuff like how to brush her teeth or how to go to work and act like The Great Therapist In The Sky or how to get some jerky guy to fuck her. I mean things that actually matter, like that I exist and I'm stuck down here in this fucking dungeon and my life is shit and her life is shit and she is a Fucking Bitch.

Statute of limitations. Or is it a statue of limitations? That's like something standing in one place and you can walk away and never look back and you're done with it. Well I'm here to tell you you're never fucking done with it.

And *him*. Don't even get me started about him.

Six

For a year and a half after she went back to work, Lathsamy appeared to hold her own. Which is not to say that she got back to where she'd been before having her child, the youthful energetic woman whose life had seemed to be flowering. She worked twenty or at most twenty-five hours a week, though with Eddie in day care she could have resumed full time. There were bad days when she got Eddie fed and dressed and dropped him at the day care center, then returned home and went back to bed until it was time to pick him up. The type of work she did gave her a lot of flexibility, not just in how many cases to take but how to organize her time, and unless she had to appear in court it was up to her how much or how little to work on any given day. I wondered whether she would have done better if she'd had an ordinary job with structured hours, with imposed expectations and constraints that wouldn't have given her the option to go back to bed, though the stress of having to show up every day, on top of all her other stresses, might have overwhelmed her.

Lathsamy's biggest struggle was with self-injury. In spite of many strategies she devised it became a kind of addiction. There were so many levels to this, suffering within suffering, the knowing infliction of harm to herself, the secrecy and shame, the powerlessness to stop, the ways that it actually helped her to cope, her unwavering belief that cutting was a way of shielding her child from her worst self.

Still, many aspects of Lathsamy's life during this period were completely normal. How different was she, actually, from lots of new mothers who struggle with the demands of parenting and work and marriage and self-care? The statistics on post-partum depression run at ten to fifteen percent, hardly a rare phenomenon. Yes, in her case this was complicated by the severity of her history, her trauma. But it seemed at the time that she was coping as well as many new mothers, bad days and self-injury notwithstanding. I felt it was important not to pathologize Lathsamy by viewing everything in her life through the lens of posttraumatic stress. I wanted to value the many ways that she was continuing to overcome her history and to live a normal life as a parent, a partner, a working adult, a spiritual person, a woman who cared deeply about the suffering of others.

Lathsamy tried hard to view herself in this same light, really to honor herself as someone whose recovery was an organically unfolding process, and I think that had a lot to do with her response when she saw a notice for a conference in Boston about sex trafficking. Which was to contact the conference organizers and offer to speak as a survivor of childhood sex slavery. They met with her and agreed.

"I can do this, Becky," she told me. "I feel it in my body. They planned the conference with no voice for survivors. How could they do that? I can make it right. This is something I can give. We can't stay invisible! Someone has to step up. I feel this is my mission."

She believed that making a public statement would be good for her psychological health and spiritual growth. She felt she had something indispensable to contribute. She spoke to me with passion; for the first time in years I felt that fire in her. At the time, and I say this despite everything that happened afterward, it so much seemed like the right thing for her to be doing.

Three weeks before the conference, in early April, Lathsamy started to feel agitated; her heart was racing and she had chest pains that didn't subside. It was a Sunday and she went to an emergency room. Her EKG was normal, but when a conscientious ER doctor ordered a C-T scan of her chest, a dark spot turned up just below her left lung. A second scan, this one of her abdomen, showed that the original dark spot was the tip of a huge tumor growing out of her kidney.

She was referred to a surgeon at Beth Israel, one of several world class hospitals in Boston. The surgeon believed that the tumor had started growing at birth and had gone undetected all this time. An MRI found cysts in her other kidney and her lungs, nothing that needed intervention for now. But obviously the massive tumor had to come out. It was very likely benign, though they couldn't be sure until it was removed, and their protocol was not to do a biopsy when there was no question of the need for surgery. The procedure would take six hours and was expected to require the removal of her kidney, maybe other organs. It was scheduled for mid-June.

Naturally it was a shock. Naturally it brought up for Lathsamy the many ways that her body had been brutalized and while there was no indication that the tumor was caused by her abuse, still it all resonated and we talked about this being one more terrible thing happening to her body that she was helpless to prevent. But she was more determined than ever to speak at the conference. She refused to let the tumor take that away from her.

At the conference, Lathsamy was the first speaker of the afternoon. During our session the day before she kept getting up and pacing around my office, something I had never seen her do. She had reached a razor sharp awareness of what it meant to go public, how much she would be exposing herself, an uncovering of raw nerves, scar tissue, wounds only partially healed. Most of the people in the room would be total strangers. Media were expected. Several of her colleagues, attorneys and social workers, had told her they planned to attend, as well as a judge from the Boston Juvenile Court where Lathsamy practiced. How would she be received? Would she be taken seriously, fully respected by the other speakers on the afternoon panel? By the conference attendees? These were understandable concerns, but at a deeper level she was confronting the most basic questions of safety and trust, of her capacity to take action in the world, to be a grown woman who was in effect carrying in her own arms her younger self for public display.

I rescheduled my afternoon appointments so I could go to the conference. When I got there the after-lunch session was about to start, people were filing into the hall and Lathsamy was already up at the front, standing and talking to a man in a gray suit. She was wearing a dark blue sinh, the conventional mid-calf length with the last two inches above the hemline an embroidered pattern in rows of light green, white and shades of blue. Her black hair was pulled back into a braid. Her body looked taut, her face tense. I found a seat about fifteen rows from the front and I tried to catch her eye but couldn't. The hall filled quickly, mostly women, many of them young. Then the man in the suit who had been talking to Lathsamy went up to the microphone and introduced her as a trafficking survivor, a witness. On behalf of the conference organizers, he expressed his gratitude that she had come forward and offered to speak.

Lathsamy walked stiffly to the podium, clutching papers in one hand. She had written out her speech, had practiced reading it to me, to Jeffrey, to her mirror. It was a recitation of the facts of her history, the sequence of events, a little dry and detached in the tone, as if the events themselves were so charged and unbearable that the language in which they were told had to be muted. I thought that wasn't necessarily a bad thing, there was an aspect of self-protection in this for Lathsamy.

Now as she started she spoke in a monotone, her eyes fixed on the prepared text. "I was born in a small village in Laos," she read. "When I was nine years old I was sold to a sex trafficking ring in Thailand." Two sentences and then she stopped. She looked up, took a breath, let it out. "This is really scary," Lathsamy said in a different voice, one in which her emotion was controlled but present. "Actually it's terrifying. Standing in front of so many people to tell my story. But it is deeply important for you to know the truth. Important enough for me to take the risk of being here and speaking to you. There is so much at stake. So many lives. So here is the truth. It was my oldest brother who dragged me across the border and sold me into slavery in Bangkok. The men gave him money. After that day I never saw my family again. I was a little girl. I knew nothing about sex. I knew nothing about the kind of men who would control my life for the next three years. Here is what they did to me. To me and to many many other girls like me. First they locked me in a room. They fed me nothing for three days. I was begging them for food. Then they started raping me. Two, three, four, five men. They told me they would feed me if I did as I was told. After they raped me they did feed me. They used food as a reward. By that time I already was a wild animal. I would do anything for food. That was one of their main ways of controlling me all the time I was in Bangkok. That and brute force."

As she spoke I could see an easing of the tension in Lathsamy's face and body. She was looking out at us in the audience with expressive, searching eyes. At some point she must have put down the papers on which she had prepared her speech, I didn't even notice her do it, what I noticed eventually was how she was gesturing as if the grace with which she was telling her story was flowing into her hands.

She told about her years in Bangkok and I thought that for many people in attendance this was the expected part of the speech, terrible in so many different ways but also conforming to what they already at some level understood about sex trafficking. What Lathsamy was giving them was not so much information about powerlessness and the inhumanity of the men, her captors and their clients, the endless degradations of the body and the spirit, but more that she was putting a human face on these things that abstractly they already knew, a living person standing before them to say look at me, these things were done to me, I was a little girl and this was my life.

She described her so-called benefactor, her escape from the trafficking ring, the international adoption and then she said, "I want to tell you about my time in the United States. As a teenager, as a young woman. I want to tell you about silence. The silence here was so vast it swallowed me whole. No one knew my story. No one wanted to know. Before long I didn't know either. I disappeared. You need to understand, this is what keeps them going. Silence, denial, make believe. The traffickers rely on it. They feed on it. It's their bullet proof vest. Don't look, don't tell, don't know. Until one day I was a grown woman and I couldn't not look anymore. I couldn't not know. People talk about breaking silences. But you can't break something that is already broken. This vast silence is the most broken thing in the world. What we need is not to do more breaking. We need to speak the truth and know that truth is a path to peace and recovery. Truth shines light on our human core and helps us to regain our wholeness. There are so many possibilities in this very moment, and the next moment, and the moment after that. Peace and safety and dignity are there in every moment, waiting for us, if we only have the courage to raise our voices and invite them into our hearts. Thank you."

Women around me were in tears. I was in tears. As Lathsamy finished we all stood.

Though I wasn't there in the morning, I knew from the program that the conference had started with a keynote by the state's Attorney General, then talks by a victim advocate, a prosecutor, a representative from the police department. All of them would have addressed the problem from the outside, how to intervene to rescue girls and women, how to find and shut down the trafficking rings. But now Lathsamy had spoken from the inside and it was exactly what she had said to me, how crucial it was to bring the raw felt reality of the experience into the conference, and after we sat down I could feel the effects of her talk still pulsing through the room. I was so proud of her, I wanted to lean toward one of the women near me and say she's my client, which of course I never would have done.

After the other presenters had given their talks, each of them making a point of saying how moved they had been by Lathsamy's testimony, there was a long Q&A session with the entire panel. Many of the questions were for Lathsamy and she handled them with the same eloquence she had emanated during her speech. At one point a young woman got up and spoke in a quivering voice about the untold thousands of ruined lives; she called it an obscenity that sex trafficking could still be happening. Where was the outrage, where were the resources, where was the needed response? Then she said that she herself had been a victim of childhood sexual abuse. Lathsamy looked directly at her, agreed that so much more was needed, that conferences like this one only mattered if they were steps toward action—and then she added that we should not be too quick to assume that lives were ruined. "I'm here as living proof that recovery is possible," she said. "I am a practicing attorney. I'm married, I have a wonderful husband and a beautiful little boy. I want no one ever to go through what I've been through. I still face big challenges. But I'm really okay."

In that moment I believed she really was okay. I knew that Lathsamy's challenges—her struggles with parenting and depression and self-injury, the iron grip of trauma and loss, the huge tumor on her kidney and the looming perils of major surgery—I knew that none of these realities had been erased by a single moment of triumph. But it was such a shining moment, and that she was capable of elevating herself in the face of so many challenges, not just the number but even more the depth of them—that, it seemed to me at the time, was as close as any of us comes to being okay.

At the end of the afternoon, people were milling in the lobby and I spotted Lathsamy standing with Jeffrey and a woman I didn't know. I made my way across, intending to congratulate her but as I approached I could see that she was in distress, her hands shaking, her eyes darting around. What could have happened? Where was the poised, centered, inspirational woman who had just addressed the conference? "They're here," she said to me. "I can feel them. They're onto these events. Every single one. It's what they do. They have a network in every city. We aren't allowed to speak. No exceptions. It's how they keep it going. I know them. I have to be punished now.

You see that door? They're waiting for me on the other side. When I step out onto the street, they're going to shoot me."

After the conference I received a steady stream of calls and emails from Jeffrey expressing mounting concern about Lathsamy. Around the time they got married Lathsamy had given me permission to talk to Jeffrey; she and I both felt this was a good idea, in case she ran into rough patches, though back then neither of us anticipated how much she might unravel. Through the hard times after Eddie's birth I heard from Jeffrey now and then, but he had been steadfast, close to unshakable in his belief that Lathsamy would pull through. Now he was overwhelmed, at a loss.

For the next two weeks Lathsamy was in a state of terror. I heard this from Jeffrey and eventually saw it for myself. She barely slept. She paced her apartment. She couldn't work. She believed her phone was bugged, her email was being hacked. She didn't go out for fear she would be shot on the street. She believed that Jeffrey was a Secret Service agent. She believed that if the traffickers had not already killed her there must be a reason, that she was being kept alive for a purpose, to be made an example of. She was terrified they would do something to Eddie. During the night she kept checking to make sure he was still there, still breathing. She didn't want the boy taken to pre-school, she and Jeffrey fought about it, until Jeffrey finally came up with the idea of having Eddie stay with his grandparents. Lathsamy agreed because, for reasons very different than Jeffrey's, she believed her child would be safer with her in-laws. Then she was frantic with him away, desperately wanted to call to talk to him but felt she couldn't because of the tapped phone line, wanted to go see him but was sure that if she did she would either be killed by the traffickers or trailed and then they would know where Eddie was. She was stranded in her own panic.

Despite everything Lathsamy kept her next appointment with me. All the way to my office she felt her life was at risk but she came anyway, needing to warn me that I was also in danger. She couldn't do this by phone or email and she also believed electronic surveillance devices had been installed in my office, so she literally whispered in my ear. I wanted so badly to reassure her, to help her calm down and realistically assess her situation, but I couldn't find anything to say that seemed at all useful. Besides, she didn't come to listen, only to whisper her desperate warnings, her belief that her own life would end any day, her unbearable dread of what might be done to her child. What I really wanted to do was to hold her, which of course I couldn't, not just because of professional boundaries but, more to the point, because I thought that physical contact would terrify her that much more. I felt helpless, as I imagined Jeffrey feeling.

I was reluctant to dismiss all of her fears as paranoia—I still am. There was to begin with the raw truth that her terrors were grounded in the reality of what had been done to her as a child. How do you tell someone who had every inch of her young life controlled by monstrous men that her current fears are exaggerated? How to tell past from present? What do I know, really, about how trafficking rings operate, what they are capable of? It wasn't impossible that they had sent someone to keep tabs on the conference, maybe not even implausible. In an age when revelations of far flung surveillance schemes have become commonplace, how could I say I was sure her phone and computer weren't being monitored? Even my office? The problem was that Lathsamy had taken these possibilities and spun them into certainties, extended them into delusions such as Jeffrey being a government agent, and she was showing classic signs of mania—her agitation, inability to sleep, racing thoughts, frantic energy, her insistent interpretation of all events through the lens of fear.

A week later when Lathsamy came to my office she sat down, looked right at me, and said out loud, "I'm frightened I'm losing touch with reality." She told me she had heard the radio talking to her, telling her what to say, what to do, speaking in a code known only to her. Somehow this jolted her into recognizing how far she had careened into dysfunction, and her healthy self managed to regain a toehold. It was like a fever breaking.

Over the next month, Lathsamy came back from the brink and held herself together. She started acupuncture and it seemed to calm her down. She resumed chanting, after having been too agitated to sit still following the conference, and then she went further, organizing what her Buddhist practice called tosos, members of her study group joining with her to chant for long periods of time. She was able to take in the reality that so far she and her family had not been killed or harmed. Eddie came back home. She began to shift some of her focus to her upcoming surgery, now less than a month away. She asked her Buddhist friends to chant for her tumor to be benign, for the surgery to be successful, for her to regain her spiritual footing and have compassion for herself and Jeffrey and Eddie.

Lathsamy had her operation the second week of June. It was a massive procedure. The surgical team was able to remove all of the tumor. It was benign, as expected. They also had to take out her left kidney, her spleen, and two adrenal glands.

Jeffrey called at the end of the afternoon to give me this mostly good news. But then he added that he had been waiting in Lathsamy's room when she was wheeled in from recovery, and as he approached her, wanting to offer support, she snapped at him in a dry brittle voice, "Don't look at me. Don't touch me. Don't stay in the room. I need to be alone."

He left, was sitting in a little waiting area at the end of the hall. He was stunned, frightened. He told me he didn't know what to do.

Seven

I decided to try on one decision or the other, day by day, the way you might shop for shoes. I would get up in the morning and tell myself I was going to have the child, try to go through the day picturing myself with a baby, all the things in my life that would change, how I would manage work, what I would do for child care, me peering over the side of a crib, me changing diapers, feeding, the feel of a small warm body next to mine, all the detailed realities of the choice. I tried it on, searching for how it felt, whether I could hold onto it, not just the images but behind them the sense of this being the actual course I was setting, grasping for the thing that could turn it into a conviction. And what I found, each time, was that I recoiled. It didn't feel like a choice, motherhood. It felt like something I wasn't capable of.

So then I would try on the abortion. Same routine, I visualized myself going to appointments at the clinic, the pre-procedure counseling, finally bringing myself to tell Hannah, having her come with me on the day, the standard medical room, the efficient medical people, competent, not necessarily uncaring, how quickly it all happens after taking so long to get there, the reality of it being over with, the post-procedure counseling, the kindness in Hannah's eyes, the feel of her hand over mine, the relief of a decision finally having been made, a life to get on with, a grief to carry. The problem, every time, was what I'd left out, the simple truth that what happens on that day is the taking of a life. It's a choice I've known women to make, clients, friends, and I have always respected that they were doing what was right for them. But it was not something I felt capable of.

Meanwhile there was the question of whether I was going to keep fucking going to my mother's house for dinner on Sundays. I really didn't want to, not after what happened the last time. But I knew that not going would create its own drama, the recriminations and rage from my mother, my father not able to make things better, and then there was Thanksgiving coming up. Did I really want to skip the next few Sundays and go through whatever would happen with my mother on the phone, which would be sure to make things worse, and then walk in for Thanksgiving with tension sky high and on top of that having to deal with my brother and his family? It was always something to be gotten through, and now I was going to subject myself to all the extra shit my mother would be sure to pile on because I'd had the gall to act like an adult and stop coming for Sunday dinner? No, I was not going to subject myself to all that extra shit. This was at least one decision I was capable of making.

But what I didn't anticipate, and really was not prepared for, was the emotional place I found myself in when I was there on those Sunday evenings. I would get to the house, my stomach in knots, my heart pounding, feeling like it was the last place I wanted to be and I was giving in to my mother one more time—and it was always about her needs and her being in charge and me being unseen and disregarded and having no fucking control. Then I'd walk in the door and it was like a switch got flipped. I'd go calm, it was eerie, and for the rest of the evening everything would just roll off me. Without any conscious effort, each of those Sundays, I checked out. Whatever my mother said, her tone of voice with its raw jagged edges, her insatiable need, the undercurrents between my parents, my father's haplessness, how much he drank, even my mother calling me Rebecca—nothing touched me. Never in my life had I failed to react to my mother's shit, to the shambles of my parents' marriage, and that alarmed me more than if I were reacting as usual. I didn't recognize myself.

* * *

Doing my work I felt normal and it was a great relief, really the only haven left in my life. When I saw my clients I could put away my stuff and while my stuff had drastically evolved over the last two months, the putting aside was nothing new. This is what you do if you're a good therapist, you recognize your own issues and you deal with them on your own time, you make sure not to impose them onto your clients, you clear your mind and your heart and make yourself fully available to the other person. I was grateful I could do that, for my sake and for my clients, but as soon as I left the office it was like I became a different person, a seriously troubled woman who was stumbling around in a life crisis without a center from which to take my bearings and chart a course.

Uncentered. I was falling apart, watching myself splinter into different selves, the competent empathic therapist, the petulant childish overwhelmed client, the angry numbed out daughter, the baffled woman incapable of making a choice, and beneath all of those fragments, something else, some other self or fragment of self, buried, driving me in an unknown direction, driving me crazy.

I started thinking that I should find a real therapist. I thought this but did nothing to make it happen.

November 10

BECKY THERAPIST: *I have an idea.*

BECKY CLIENT: *About time.*

BT: *I think there may have been trauma in your past, most likely during childhood...*

BC: *I already told you what happened when I was eight.*

BT: *Yes, something else.*

BC: What, you don't think that was a trauma? I spilled my fucking guts to you about how my mother treated me and it wasn't just that one afternoon when I was eight, you know, it was all along. I tried to tell you this and you keep saying that you hear me but do you? Really? The whole point is that she never loved me for myself, she only ever wanted me to be the person she imagined me to be, she only ever wanted me to take care of her and that is still going on, a whole lifetime of not getting anything that matters from my mother and that's not enough for you?

BT: That completely counts, the love and acceptance you never have gotten from your mother, it's a huge trauma and it has caused such deep suffering in your life.

BC: So?

BT: I think there may be something else.

BC: Why?

BT: Because you're having symptoms that often come from being violated in a certain way.

BC: Like what?

BT: Dissociation...

BC: Plain English.

BT: The way you're numbing out when you have dinner with your parents. How easily you can shut off your bad feelings when you go to work. The way you're fragmenting into different selves that seem disconnected from each other. The sense you have of something buried, something inside that you can't get hold of.

BC: Okay, so this is supposed to mean that I was violated

in a certain way.

BT: It could mean that, yes.

BC: In what way?

BT: Something done to your body.

BC: You think I was raped.

BT: Something like that.

BC: What do you mean, something like that?

BT: Some type of sexual abuse. There's a continuum...

BC: You think I was raped when I was a girl and I've blocked it out.

BT: It's possible.

BC: Like Lathsamy.

BT: Like Lathsamy in the sense...

BC: You think I was a sex slave like Lathsamy.

BT: I think it's very unlikely that you were ever involved in sex trafficking like Lathsamy. What could be similar is the way she blocked out what happened to her. It's common to lose memories of childhood sexual abuse.

BC: And you think the same thing would happen to me as happened to Lathsamy when she had her baby, is that it? You think that's what I'm really scared of?

BT: Possibly...

BC: So Lathsamy is just hanging out there as my, what would you call it, negative role model? I was raped and I don't remember just like Lathsamy. Having a baby will fuck me up just like Lathsamy.

BT: It doesn't have to be exactly like Lathsamy...

BC: Look, let's say this is all true, I mean we're talking

about speculation on top of speculation but just saying—how in the world does it help me to make a decision? So we take my mother out of the equation and replace her with Lathsamy. Or we leave Mom in and just add Lathsamy to the mix, and all I want is to not be like my mother and to not repeat Lathsamy's mistakes because it turns out that I am so much like her? What does this tell me that I don't already know? I already know I don't want the baby. I already know I don't want an abortion. I already know my life is shit and I am utterly incapable of dealing with the mess I've made for myself. Where does this leave me that isn't the exact fucking place I was already in?

When I was in graduate school, my father was a featured speaker at a conference in Boston on psychopathology in adolescent girls. I wasn't sure until the last minute whether I could make it to the conference, and when I did finally register I decided it would be fun to surprise him by showing up. He gave a talk in the morning on how to differentiate personality disorders from normal teenage rebellion. This was during a plenary session and I sat near the back of the auditorium, so he still didn't know I was there.

The gist of his speech was that we shouldn't be too quick to see pathology in adolescents, a kind of rule of thumb should be to assume them normal until proven otherwise. He said this was especially true for girls, with our unfortunate history of double standards about sexual activity and any kind of assertiveness. I was pleased that he highlighted how sexism could come into play, not usually his strong suit, but the great thing about his talk was how he gave it, his ease, his command of the material. The large hall was about three-fourths full, there must have been over two hundred people and from where I was sitting my father was a small figure up on the stage, but above and behind him was a large screen and since Dad wasn't using a power point, someone had a camera trained on him and his image was projected up on the screen. It gave him an aura of being larger than life. He had notes at the podium but he rarely referred to them, and with a hand-held mic he paced the stage the way some professors do when they lecture, it conveyed his energy and enthusiasm. In the big image on the screen we could see his tongue brush against his lip as he gathered himself to deliver his next idea, how he narrowed one eye and not the other, there was almost an intimacy to it. He was sharing with us only a sliver of the knowledge and wisdom he had accumulated over a long, fruitful professional career; in the audience you could feel this and it wasn't only because I was his daughter.

My father was in his early sixties then, at the height of his intel-lectual powers. I had seen him speak a number of times before and I was always struck by the difference between his public and private persona, but never more than on that day. At home he either faded into the woodwork, completely overshadowed by my mother's huge emotional presence, or else he was reaching the end of his rope and getting into some kind of ugly, useless confrontation with her. But in a professional setting he was in his element, sure of himself, quick on his feet, engaging, vital. I sat there feeling proud and more than that, I just felt such deep appreciation and love for my dad.

A luncheon was part of the conference and I felt sure I would find him there, since he was scheduled to lead a workshop right afterward. I walked into a large room with its round tables, already crowded and buzzing, waitpeople scooting around and beginning to serve people who were seated. I looked around and spotted him at the far side of the room, the elegant impeccably dressed white haired man. As I made my way toward him I was scanning his table for an empty seat, and then my attention shifted to the woman sitting next to my father. She looked familiar, around my age, her dark hair tied back in a ponytail, a button nose and eager attentive eyes, and as I got closer I recognized her from school, she had been in one of my classes and I thought I remembered her name was Jill. She and my father were talking, he was animated and she was smiling at him and yes, it could just have been that she was a young admirer but the energy I was

picking up between them felt pretty weird. My father didn't notice
me until I was almost right next to him, but then he flashed me a look
of delighted surprise and got up and gave me a big hug. People moved
around so I could sit on one side of him, the woman was still on his
other side and I was right, her name was Jill. It turned out that she
was interning at a residential program for disturbed children where
my father consulted, reason enough for them to be sitting together.

I might have left it at that, but after Dad's workshop he asked me if
we could go for a walk. We strolled down Massachusetts Avenue, the
section between Boylston Street and Symphony Hall, chatting about
the conference, what I thought of his talk, ideas that came up during
the discussion at his workshop. Cars streamed past, a bus spewed its
dark exhaust. We passed a construction area on our left, the sidewalk
narrowed and was bordered by a fence, then we came to Christian
Science Plaza with its huge domed church and the long rectangular
reflecting pool that glistened in the afternoon sun. By the pool my
father stopped, turned toward me, raised a hand to his forehead to
shield his eyes. "Becky," he said, "I want to be up front about this,
Jill and I are having an affair."

I wasn't surprised after what I had seen but I was stunned, he
must have read it in my face and he added, "Your mother knows, I
wouldn't do something like this and not be open about it." He told
me it wasn't his first affair. He told me he and Mom hadn't had sex in
twenty years. He said he and Mom had an understanding, his freedom
to have these encounters with other women was a way of keeping their
marriage together. He said he wasn't sure Mom could manage without
him. "Before this I never saw any reason for you—well, I didn't think
I should burden you with it. But now, I mean you saw us together. I
thought I should tell you."

I don't remember what I said. I do remember what I felt. I was
grateful he hadn't told me before then. I was grateful he did tell me
that day, rather than leaving me wondering what the hell was going on
between him and Jill. Naturally I noticed that he was involved with a

woman less than half his age and I curbed my feelings, my judgments, telling myself that he was hardly the first man in his sixties to have an affair with a woman in her twenties. I didn't have a clue why he would think my mother would need him in order to manage. More than anything, once I got over the shock, I was truly glad for him that he had this happening in his life. These intimacies, however weird or limited they might be, were some version of joy that he hadn't lost entirely to a horrible marriage.

Now, thirteen years later, I was thinking about my father's sexual behavior and it was creeping me out. An aging man sleeping with a woman almost forty years younger. What else was he capable of? What else didn't I know about him?

Creeping me out. What did that even mean? I was probing myself for something familiar and certain, a floor or even a basement, a place to bottom out that I could look to and say, things are bad and may get worse but no worse than this—and I couldn't find it.

I also started thinking about my own sexual behavior and it was disturbing me almost as much as my father's.

I started being sexually active when I was fifteen, went out with a good number of boys in high school and lots in college, some of them for long enough to call boyfriends but nothing really close to serious, and some I thought of as adventures. I liked to get high when I had sex, on alcohol or pot or both. None of this was especially out of the ordinary for that age, yes there were girls who had steady boyfriends or girlfriends and others who didn't seem to go out much, but many of the girls I knew were cycling in and out of relationships or having one nighters. At least that was the story I told myself, and there was enough truth to it for me to pass over, in my own view of myself, the venom I felt for the boys I slept with. When my friends and I talked about how guys sucked, it could mean a hundred different things, and looking back I had pretty much no curiosity about what it actually meant for me, the intensity of my feelings.

During my second year of grad school I somehow managed to

be with the same man for ten months, something you could almost describe as a relationship. Gary, also a second year student, a nice guy. We hung out on weekends, liked the same kinds of movies, had interesting conversations. He was the one man I saw who didn't end up repulsing me, but at the same time there was no real spark. We were more like friends who had sex. After graduation he got a job in Seattle which was where he was from. We parted on good terms and there was never any question of me moving out there with him, let alone asking him to stay in Boston.

Then I reverted to the old pattern, the long succession of sex partners, men I met at parties or bars or, more recently, through online dating services, men I would sleep with once or a few times or in some cases for a few months but never longer, men I needed to get drunk or stoned with in order to have sex, men who I always ended up regarding as boring or pretentious or shut down or crass or self-centered or just plain ugly. Some of them, men whose names I can't remember.

And now, looking back at this sorry trail of heartless sex and disconnection, now in this moment when I was finding myself so much lacking a center, with this terrible hanging question about what might have happened to me as a child, about the person my father really was and what he could have done to me, I was startled to look at my own behavior as an adolescent, as an adult, at patterns that were so painfully clear but I had been ignoring for over twenty years, and I was flooded with questions for which I had no good answers. Why was I attracted to men who were assholes? Why did I endlessly repeat the same stupid choices? Why had I been so completely unaware of the failure, the self-destructiveness of my sex life? Why did I learn nothing from experience? Why, if I had such a dismal view of men, did I keep seeking them out? Why, if I had such a good relationship with my father, if I admired and loved him so much, and if as I believed a girl's relationship with her father creates the foundation for healthy or unhealthy adult relationships, why was I disgusted by almost every man I'd ever slept with?

The man in my first nightmare didn't look like my father but there was something familiar about him. The scene kept changing and he kept being there, a barn, a busy sidewalk, a room in a house with old shabby furniture, he was a big burly man with a thick mustache and red coarse hands and I was a girl, I don't know how old but I felt very little next to his bigness. Then we are in a bar and what's familiar is the smell of alcohol on his breath and he is walking toward me and I want to get away from him but I can't move. I'm frozen even before he touches me and I feel panic rising like nausea through my small body, my heart is pounding and I'm breathing fast and he is above me and he puts one big hand on my forehead, I want to squirm but I can't even do that and then with his other hand he covers my mouth and I can't breathe and I wake up gasping for air.

November 16

BECKY CLIENT: *Okay I do not like where this is going, all this stuff about my father and yes I had a nightmare and the man smelled of alcohol and I was terrified when he put his hand over my mouth and if I hadn't woken up he probably would have raped me. I accept all that. I accept that I associate the smell of alcohol with my father. But that dream could have meant a thousand different things. I associate alcohol with my father but how many fucking men have I slept with who smelled of alcohol? Why my father and not one of them? And sure the guy had a mustache but it wasn't anything like Dad's mustache. Nothing else about him was the least bit like Dad, so why focus on the things that are like Dad and say this was about him, why not focus on all the things about the guy that weren't like Dad and say this must have been about something else? Why try to figure out* what it meant in the first place when there is no way to be sure?

BECKY THERAPIST: So in the dream you were terrified and were probably about to be raped. But it sounds like what's really important to you is not to assume that the man in the dream was your father.

BC: Right, and this whole thing about me being raped— you tell me that I'm having the kind of symptoms someone has who was sexually abused when she was little and I'm blocking out what happened to me—and then poof!—I have this dream. How fucking convenient. What's to say this isn't power of suggestion? What's to say I didn't just have a bad dream and it doesn't mean anything at all? What makes you so high and mighty? What gives you the right to declare what happened to me and what my father did or didn't do when you don't know any more about it than me?

BT: I'm hearing you say that the whole thing could have been the power of my suggestion or might just have been a bad dream that didn't mean anything. And it sounds like you're really angry at me for suggesting that you might have been sexually abused when you were little.

BC: Yes! And you're probably going to say that it's just fine and dandy for me to be angry at you.

BT: Yes.

BC: Yeah, right....And then the other thing about my father having affairs and sleeping with women my age and how creepy it is and suddenly we're seeing him in a whole different light—well sure it's creepy, but it doesn't mean...

This gathering of evidence and reconstructing history, you know the veil lifting and suddenly we see my father as he really is and what he really is, is a monster. Well I am not ready to say that my father is a monster.

BT: To you, your father is not a monster. It sounds like you have such deep feelings about this.

BC: I just feel like where all this is leading is for me to have to give up my father, to give up the man I have known and loved all my life, as though that holds the key to everything, and I am not about to do that. I can't stand it that I'm having these suspicions about him. I don't even know who I would be without my father. I just need him to be who he is.

Part II

Thanksgiving

Here's a good one—who's a bigger asshole, the FB or me? You might think it's a no-brainer, but take a look at me and what do you see? A pathetic sniveling little piece of shit, that's what. I'm a little fucking bitch! Her and me, two peas in a fucking pod, Big Becky and little becky and the both of us deserve every single bad thing that happens to us, and yes I spelled little becky with little letters just to be cute even though I know it's not the least bit funny.

Do you think I like being like this? Do you think I like the things I say, all the fucking suffering I cause? I can't help it! She made me like this, I didn't even choose to be alive, I hate being alive, I am her fucking prisoner and she brings all this onto her own stupid self and I don't have a choice about anything.

But once I was up there, out in the sunlight, there was a time when I was her for real and I was an actual human being and not this weird twisted piece of shit that I am now. How did this happen? I can't even tell you who I was and I cannot tell you who I could have been or who she could have been. We were just little and we had our whole life ahead of us and there was no wizard behind the curtain and there was no little monster causing all this pain, and look at who we are now and look at what our life has become and how can this be and...

Fuck this shit. I can't even stand the sound of my own voice.

Eight

My next two nightmares were classics. In the first one I was driving a car from the back seat, leaning forward and extending my arms to reach the steering wheel and for some time I was driving along at a normal speed on a city street. Cars came toward me and passed on the other side of the road, on my side there was traffic at a safe distance in front. It seemed perfectly ordinary that I should be driving from the back and I felt in control of the car, I wasn't even thinking about my feet until I went to slow down and I couldn't reach the brake. I tried to extend my legs the same as my arms and I couldn't, I kept jamming my foot into the bottom of the front seat and suddenly it comes into focus, obvious, I'm in the back seat and there is no way to reach the brake. The road is sloping and the car is speeding up, I'm bearing down on a blue Toyota Corolla in front of me, I need to slow down and I can't and I swerve and I'm going faster and I keep reaching for the brake, there's a curve ahead and I jam my foot into the seat harder and I know it's impossible but if I push fiercely enough with my foot it's got to work. I have to reach the brake and I can't, I can't, I'm into the curve and my heart is pounding, I feel myself careening and I wake up.

Two nights later I dreamed that I was walking into an apartment building and up the stairs, down a hallway to where I stopped and knocked on a door, the door opened and there was a man I didn't know, a tall man with dark hair and a large nose and red blotchy cheeks. I couldn't remember why I was there and then I realized all I was wearing was a shirt, I tried to pull it down but it only went as far as my navel so I tried to act normal, I thought he won't notice but he did notice, I thought this can't be happening but it was.

Driving home from Sunday dinners I kept finding myself picturing my father having sex with Jill. Him on top, him on bottom, my father naked and in bed with this very young woman, I would shudder and try to get the images out of my head and for a moment they would stop. I would just begin to let my guard down and then another image would pop up, my father with a different woman, even younger than Jill at the time, someone I had never actually seen and I would tell myself I was only imagining this and I would answer, in a dialogue in my head that I couldn't stop any more than the images—I would ask if this truly was only something I was imagining. The specific image, yes, but my father has had many affairs and he obviously has a taste for young women; if Jill at twenty-five then why not another one even younger? Who knew what his boundaries were, or if he had boundaries?

I thought of him sitting with me in the living room, chatting about politics or climate change, or with my mother and me at the dinner table, and I would try to bring myself back to this external reality and believe that nothing was actually different. He was still the elegant older man who made incisive comments, drank another glass of wine, flew under Mom's radar, was just as kind and accepting of me as ever. I told myself that I should be having angst about my mother and it's not like I wasn't, but it kept getting shoved aside by the dread I was feeling about my father. I couldn't retreat into the old comforting version of my dad, couldn't shake the images and doubts out of my head, couldn't stop wondering what he did to me, couldn't believe he was a perpetrator, couldn't convince myself that he wasn't.

I dreamed I was camping in a clearing in a dense forest. It's night, I sit in front of my campfire, alone. Surrounding the dancing fire there is darkness, silence. No moon, no wind. Above, the vast night sky. I hear something rustle behind me, faint, distant. The first breath of breeze, I think. It sounds again, closer, more distinct, only from one spot, too isolated, too low to the ground to be wind through the leaves. An animal. What? I riffle through the possibilities, chipmunk, porcupine, skunk, coyote, raccoon. Again, louder, something large, moving steadily and then he bursts into the clearing. I turn around and see the bear, I feel his maleness in my body and watch as he rears up onto his hind legs, huge against the dim outline of the forest, his big cock sticking out. I stand to face him, not knowing why, not intending to run, not intending to fight, not intending anything. The fire is behind me now, I feel its warmth radiating up my legs, butt, spine, the cold of the night in my face and now wind is blowing through my hair, I feel loose strands tossed onto my cheeks, my neck, I am all sensation and my mind is blank. The bear approaches, with one swipe he tears off my jacket, with another he rips my shirt, he paws at my breasts and I stand there with nowhere to go. I look up and see flames leaping in his eyes and then he pushes and I stagger and trip and fall backward into the fire.

November 21

BECKY CLIENT: *I don't even know what my crisis is anymore.*

BECKY THERAPIST: *Can you say what you mean?*

BC: *When I started talking to you everything was clear cut. It's not like life was great, it was horrible and I didn't know what to do and of course I still don't know what to do, but back then there was one crappy decision I couldn't make. Now I'm creeped out about my father, and I'm creeping myself out, and I don't know what did or didn't happen to me. I feel like there's all this stuff inside me that I don't know* and all this mess is my fault. I feel like I have lived my whole life under some kind of pretense, and I can't stop having bad thoughts, and I can't stand these fucking nightmares and now I'm scared just to go to sleep.

BT: So I'm hearing you say that when we started talking you had one very clear crisis in your life, which was not being able to decide whether to keep the child. And now it's like your crises keep multiplying and you feel out of control, you don't know what's going on inside you but you feel that whatever is wrong must be your fault, and it sounds like you're really really scared by the nightmares.

BC: And you know I've wanted to blame everything on you, I've been wanting you to be the person I could be angry at and that's completely unfair, you haven't done anything to me and I'm the one I should be angry at and I am so sorry.

BT: Is it shame you're feeling?

BC: Shame, yeah, sure, and on top of everything else I still can't decide about the baby. You know some day I'm going to start showing, I have no idea when but the way things are going it's bound to happen, that's reality, right, and then I'll be totally fucked.

BT: So it's like your pregnancy is an awful secret, and it's only a matter of time before your secret is revealed.

BC: It's like everything I touch turns to shit and I have nowhere to turn. Well except to you.

BT: Everything is falling apart, and the only place you can turn for support is our sessions.

BC: Yeah, it doesn't feel like enough, no offense, but at

least it's something. You know I should be able to do better than this. I should have some, I don't even know what to call it. Strength? Resourcefulness? Something inside myself instead of just walking around like a whimpering puppy. I mean listen to me, I'm pathetic, I'm worse than pathetic, I'm fucking useless, all I do is whine and blather. And now here I am putting myself down, that's sure to help, right?

BT: So you feel bad about feeling so helpless, and you think that expressing your feelings doesn't make anything better. But I also heard you say that you would like to find the strength and resourcefulness in yourself to be able to deal with all these overwhelming things that are happening.

BC: There is so much shit and I know I need to face it and I don't know how to do it.

In my dream I'm trying to find the Traffic & Parking Office. When I enter the building I hold the door open for a little woman with a scrunched up face wearing a long dark coat and I let her go ahead and she nods and passes. I have an ulterior motive, I'm sure she knows where she is going, and where she is going is Traffic & Parking and I will follow her. Just inside the door there is a suite of offices on one side, the rest is a mall and a large sign by the entrance to the suite lists offices by name and number and there it is, Traffic & Parking number 30, and next to it a smaller sign saying smallpox. The woman disappears into a different office and I am on my own. I walk through the suite looking at room numbers and I can't find 30 anywhere. I wander out into the mall, still looking for a door and a 30 but what I see is more smallpox signs, they get bigger and bigger SMALLPOX and I follow them to a storefront which I know is a sex establishment where a man greets me. His face is pale, his hair slicked down, he is unwell and perplexed and he says If you want smallpox I can just inject you, and I say It's not so much what I want as that I need it, and he takes out a huge syringe and plunges the needle into my chest.

* * *

I was dreading Thanksgiving, not just the day but a cluster of days starting with Tuesday when Mark and his family would arrive. That evening we would all be having dinner at my parents' house, followed by an outing to the Boston Science Museum on Wednesday afternoon, the extravaganza on Thursday, brunch on Friday. We'd been doing this same routine for years, acting as if this week were not just an annual show of obligation, as if Mark only comes to Boston once a year because he is so busy with his work, as if we were not riddled with festering conflicts, as if there were anything remotely healthy about us a family. Mom would fill the air with angst about the meals and the logistics and anything else along the way that she couldn't control down to the last detail, with breaks for her to shower overbearing adoration on her granddaughters. Mark and I would, as usual, have almost nothing to say to each other and I would watch him being distant and arrogant with our mother, watch her shore herself up over and over again to ignore his coldness and tell him how happy she is to see him, how much the girls have grown, how beautiful and lovable they are. Mark's wife, Christine, would have the same smile etched onto her face the entire time, as if she were posing for a photo, would treat all of us with the same forced graciousness. My father would find ways to make himself scarce, errands to run, phone calls, would be polite and charming when he had no means of escape, would start drinking in the afternoon.

* * *

The room in my dream is spinning. There is some sort of furniture behind me and I try to sit but find myself on the wooden floor. The man above me is twice my size, he won't keep still and I can't tell if it's because he is dancing or swaying or because nothing is keeping still,

I can't make out his face, only his bigness and I can't tell if I am little or he is big like a giant and I am normal size and it's his bigness that makes me seem small, and by the way, he smells of alcohol. Why by the way? I don't know and it seems like a silly question, I feel like a silly person and he is still there standing over me, unsteady on his feet or I am unsteady in my vision—what a funny way to put it—and now here he is on the floor next to me, this big man. You're my sweetheart, he says. Don't you want to be my sweetheart? I laugh, sweetheart, it's just the funniest thing, that I could be somebody's sweetheart, that I could be this big man's sweetheart.

His arm is draped across the top of my back, his big hand grasping me just below the shoulder and I can smell something else, his sweat, it smells gross and I like the alcohol smell better. Come on, sweetheart, he says in a booming voice, come on and I don't know what he wants me to do and the room is still spinning. I'm getting a funny feeling in the middle of my tummy and I try to move away from him and I can't. Come on, sweetheart, he keeps saying it and it's not funny anymore and I sit there next to him on the floor because there is nothing else I can do. Now I am lying flat on my back and I feel the hardness of the floorboards under my head and his big body is on top of me, his mouth on my mouth and I feel crushed and it's hard to breathe, he sticks his tongue into my mouth and it's gross and I'm too little for this and I can feel in my mind and feel in my back that it's my bed under me, it's my bed in my bedroom and I'm asleep and I know this, I am dreaming and I know it and I can't wake up. I can't move from under the weight of the big man and I can't wake up and get out of this dream, I want to and I can't and the bed and the floor are both real and there is nothing I can do to get away from him. The big man takes his mouth off my mouth, he says sweetheart again, he says you like this, he says you want me to be doing this, he says you want me to stick my thing into you, he says you are begging me to stick my throbbing thing into you. I try to say no and I can't hear my own voice and then his hand is over my mouth and his other hand is pulling down my skirt and then he is doing something else down there and something else and it's as if a huge nail is being pounded into me and I don't feel anything I don't feel it I don't I don't I don't don't don't don't don't.

November 24

BECKY CLIENT: *I'm scared.*

BECKY THERAPIST: *Because...*

BC: *Because I can't stop having nightmares. Because I can't convince myself anymore that they're only dreams. Because last night in my dream I got raped. Because I can feel in my body that it's true. Because I got raped by a big man when I was little. Because I've been living all these years with this knowledge buried in my body. Because I don't know what this means for me. Because I think I do know what it means for me. Because I don't know myself. Because I'm scared to know myself. Because I'm falling fucking apart. Because I'm scared that I'm like Lathsamy. Because I'm scared of what I've done with my life. Because I'm scared of what I haven't done with my life. Because I'm scared that I'm damaged beyond repair. Because I don't know what to do. Because I'm scared to find out who did this to me. Because I think I know. Because I don't want to know. Because my whole life has been a house of cards.*

BT: *So you're feeling deeply frightened by all the nightmares you've been having, and especially the last one of being raped. You can feel in your body that this really happened to you when you were little and that touches off so* many other fears, of having had this buried in you for so long, of being damaged, of...

BC: Okay, enough! I know you're listening, I feel fucking heard, but what about you? Sometimes I swear you sound like a fucking robot. Don't you have any feelings?

BT: Yes, of course I have feelings.

BC: Well not of course if I have to ask! Or maybe it's just me being clueless, like I seem to be clueless about everything.

BT: So you're doubting your...

BC: Stop!

BT: You don't want me to say back what I'm hearing.

BC: No!

BT: What do you want?

BC: I want you to tell me your feelings.

BT: You mean about...

BC: Yes I mean about!

BT: I feel upset. I feel furious. I feel sadder than I can say. I feel scared.

BC: How can you feel those things and be so calm?

BT: I don't really know. I just do it. I do it because you need me to be calm.

BC: You do that for me?

BT: Yes.

Nine

In the turbulent summer days and weeks following Lathsamy's surgery, Jeffrey was in touch with me more than ever, a distraught husband reporting on events as they spiraled out of control. From his accounts, from my own sessions with Lathsamy, from hospital records when she consented to have them sent to me, I gathered the story of that terrible summer.

Four days after the operation Lathsamy was sent home. During her entire stay in the hospital she was tightly coiled, in pain, ready to snap at any perceived slight. She yelled at nurses for ignoring her, yelled at doctors for not upping her pain medicine. She let Jeffrey sit in her room on condition that he not speak. On the morning of her discharge she called and told him not to bother coming to the hospital, someone from her Buddhist community was going to drive her home.

Back at home it was more of the same. She was short tempered with Jeffrey, impatient with Eddie who naturally wanted attention from his mother after she had been away for several days. A child his age could not fully understand the meaning of an operation and needed reassurance that Lathsamy was okay and still loved him, reassurance that she was not able to give. She would make brief attempts to placate the boy, start to play a game with him or read part of a picture book until her attention would wander. Eddie would get upset, she would tell him to stop bothering her and he would get more upset until Jeffrey would take the baffled little boy away, explaining that his mother was tired and needed to rest.

But Lathsamy was agitated, not tired, and she couldn't rest. She paced around the apartment, still in pain, her steps labored. The third day she insisted on going out by herself into ninety degree heat, was away for hours. When she got back she told Jeffrey she'd gone to a movie, then walked all the way home; what would normally have been a thirty minute walk took her two hours. She'd gotten dehydrated and exhausted, stopped in a store to buy a soda, then found a bench where she took a nap. She hadn't brought insulin with her, and when she tested her blood sugar at home it was sky high.

Later that week she also insisted on coming to my office for our appointment, refusing my offer to have our session on the phone. She was full of grievances, again unable to sit still. She doubted that there was any medical necessity for her organs to have been removed, suspected the tumor was malignant and the doctor had lied. She was fed up with Jeffrey, fed up with marriage, tired of being a mother, sick to death of no one knowing who she was and what she was going through and the meaning of her life. When I tried to speak, to ask for example what she felt the meaning of her life was, or to express concern about her physical condition, or simply to empathize and paraphrase what I was hearing her say, she cut me off, went on pacing and speaking rapidly in a jagged, injured voice. "Becky," she said to me at one point, "you're a nice person. Well meaning and so innocent. The things you don't know. You think you know, but you don't. I know and it isn't pretty. I'm sorry for you, Becky. I worry about you. This world is going to eat you alive, the way it eats me alive every single day. You'll get your turn. Watch your back Becky, mark my words."

Her surgical staples were scheduled to come out at the beginning of July. The evening before, Lathsamy went to a meeting of her Buddhist study group. Jeffrey got calls from two members of the group, each sounding shaken. Lathsamy had come into the meeting with a full head of steam, they told him. She announced that no one there understood the true meaning Nichiren Buddhism, that they were phonies and armchair Buddhists and dilettantes. She went on and on like this, claiming that her suffering gave her special insights and privileges, things they were too ignorant to appreciate. Both of the people who called said they were frightened for Lathsamy, that this was not the woman they knew and they feared she was having some kind of breakdown. When she walked in the door Lathsamy looked at Jeffrey and said, "They've been talking to you about me, haven't they," didn't wait for him to answer, walked off to her study and slammed the door.

The next morning she went by herself to the hospital to have her staples out, unwilling for Jeffrey go with her. At the end of the afternoon Jeffrey picked Eddie up from pre-school and came home to an empty apartment. That evening he got a call from a resident at the Beth Israel emergency room. His wife had gone to her appointment with the surgeon, the doctor told him, but then would not allow the surgeon to examine her or to remove the staples. Her behavior was erratic and the surgeon, aware of Lathsamy's mental health history, decided to send her to the ER for a psychiatric evaluation. Hospital security had to be called to accompany her to the ER. In the emergency room she was agitated, hostile, delusional and out of control. At one point she started throwing whatever she could get her hands on and had to be physically restrained. She was also medically unstable, her blood sugar fluctuating wildly, and blood work found her thyroid level, previously too low, was now abnormally elevated.

She was seen by a psychiatrist; he decided to have her hospitalized. But first she had to be stabilized medically. They held her in the ER overnight, and the next day, her blood sugar still out of control, she was moved to a bed on a medical unit.

By the time Lathsamy's blood sugar was stable, she appeared to have calmed down and was asking to be released rather than transferred to the psych unit as originally planned. Jeffrey was with her, and he later told me that she had him believing she was more or less back to her normal self. She was talking to him, seemed friendly, apologized for her behavior since her surgery. She wanted to go home to their child. When a psychiatrist came to reassess her, Lathsamy spoke in even tones, no hint of paranoia, was able to sit still. She breezed through the standard mental status exam, able to state the date, time, and place, name the last three presidents, count backwards by sevens from one hundred, explain what it means that a rolling stone gathers no moss. She had no thoughts of hurting herself or anyone else. The psychiatrist could find no grounds to hold her, and discharged her with a diagnosis of post-surgical delirium, resolved.

But something incalculably more serious than a passing delirium was happening to Lathsamy. Still in the hospital, sitting in her room with Jeffrey waiting to be discharged, she started to work herself up as thirty, sixty, ninety minutes passed and she had to wait for paperwork to be completed and prescriptions to be written, the delay as it extended becoming intolerable. By the time they got home she seemed to her husband to have fallen back into the state she had been in before her stay in the hospital, no better for it. She was infuriated at the surgeon, still believing he had botched her surgery, then had the audacity to think he had the right to touch her body when she went back to see him, then called her crazy for telling him to keep his hands off her, then summoned security to manhandle her. She was enraged at the emergency room staff who had kept her in the hospital against her will—an incarceration whatever antiseptic medical language they wanted to put on it—then physically abused her and tampered with her blood sugar to justify their abuse of power. She was going to sue the surgeon and the hospital, they didn't know who they were dealing with. When she finally asked where Eddie was, and learned that he was with Jeffrey's parents, she was incredulous, outraged, couldn't see why Jeffrey hadn't found a sitter so the boy would be there when she got home. She took it as an insult, a vote of no confidence in her as a mother and a human being, wouldn't listen when Jeffrey tried to explain, stomped away.

I offered Lathsamy an emergency appointment the next day after Jeffrey, desperate, called my cell phone that evening. Lathsamy came on the phone briefly and agreed, and I thought this at least, her willingness to see me, was a good sign. But she showed up at my office dressed in a mini skirt and tank top, the long thin scars in plain view crisscrossing her forearms and thighs, wearing thickly applied mascara and bright red lipstick and rouge, this on a face I had never seen made up; and when I greeted her as I always did she glared at me and said, "My name is Lulu."

Ten

The Tuesday before Thanksgiving. I arrive at my parents' house for our family dinner, the beginning of four days from Hell. I ring the bell and my sister-in-law Christine opens the door. She's a mousy little woman, I know that sounds pejorative but it's also true: she can't be more than five feet, skinny and small boned, wide cheeks and big eyes and permed brown hair; all that's missing is a tail. The image of her in bed with Mark, who is big, not exactly fat but burly, muscular, the two of them together in the dark, my brother's heavy weight on top of her—why would she choose a partner twice her size, how can she stand it? Barely inside the house and already I'm thinking of gruesome sex.

April, their six year old, is peeking at me from behind her mother. I say hello as warmly as I can, hang my coat in the vestibule closet, and hand April a present wrapped in blue tissue paper. She squeals and Christine says, "Oh Becky, you shouldn't have," which makes me want to gnash teeth because I emailed her about the books I was thinking to give April and to the ten year old, Martha, to make sure they hadn't already read them. April asks if she can open it now and Christine says she should ask me and I say of course. It's *Frog and Toad Together*, one of the delights of my own childhood. For Martha, an avid and advanced reader, I got *Inkheart*.

April wants me to read her new book with her, and Christine says that she and Martha are helping my mother with dinner and it would be just great if I could keep April occupied. Of course I notice that my mother will let Christine help in the kitchen but never me, this is nothing new but I have a have a flash of jealousy anyway. I tell myself that I would so much rather go read with April in the living room and that's what we do.

We settle ourselves onto the ugly green couch and April, clutching her new book in both hands, presses up against me. Her hair, two shades lighter than her mother's, is neatly parted and touches the edge of her shoulders, kept off her forehead by a clip in the shape of a bow, its color matching the lavender of her shirt and sweater, and I wonder what it means to her, the attention that goes into making her attractive, whether it is preparing her for a lifetime of winning or losing esteem for her appearance. April opens the book to the first story. I help her sound out words and we wend our way through Toad making a list of things to do and then losing it when a strong wind blows the paper out of his hand; we laugh together at Toad's dismay, how he says blah and drat and plops down in a funk because he can't do anything without his list of things to do. We have just come to the part where Frog goes chasing after Toad's list when April glances up and notices my brother's presence before I do. "Hi Daddy," she says casually.

"Hey Sweetheart," Mark says as he strides across the room toward us. "Whatcha got there?"

SWEETHEART, the word explodes over my head and in that instant my entire body is shaking, nausea is in my throat and I know everything that matters. I can hear April's voice and it's a thousand miles away and without saying anything I hoist my body off the couch and make it to the bathroom before I vomit into the sink. I don't think I can keep standing but I have to because I am still retching, I grab the sides of the sink and hold on like a drowning woman, and just when I think there can't be more there is. My body is an uproar, the roiling in my intestines, my racing heart, this shaking I cannot steady, a raging energy everywhere my fingers armpits back calves shoulders pounding through my head my thighs, and in my thighs is also an aching, a deep melancholy pain there and in my hips and my butt the base of my spine, my vulva, my tongue the roof of my mouth, and a sharp stabbing in my vagina and I know I have been holding this pain for so many years, thirty years of making myself not feel it, well I'm feeling it now and my lungs, I can't get enough air into my lungs, I am panting and they will never fill and there it is, his heavy weight on top of me, crushing my breath, crushing my pelvis, my thighs my intestines and there he is inside me I can feel him and all I want is to get him off of me, all I want is to get him out of me, I want to hurt him I want to make him feel what I feel I want to empty my body, I am my body there is nothing else and I retch one more time and I run the water and I turn it off and I let myself sink down to the floor.

I push backward until I feel the wall behind me. I lean against it and pull up my knees and wrap my arms around them, clasp my hands together and shake and hold as still as I can and breathe. I have to get the fuck out of this house, I'm a prisoner plotting her escape and the first thing is I will have to somehow find my bag, my keys. I lift up my head and look at the bathroom door and there it is, my bag, a miracle right here on the floor. I have no memory of it having been in the living room, no memory of bringing it with me in here, is there no end to this, the things I don't remember. Now I will need to make my body move, I need to pick up the bag and turn the handle to the door and move my feet and will my body to the vestibule and find my coat and pray no one sees me, but instead as I lift myself up off the floor another wave of nausea is rising and I am clutching the sink again and retching and there is nothing left to vomit and I retch and retch.

When finally it stops I look up into the mirror and see tears streaming down my cheeks and I think, I'm glad I don't wear mascara, and I think, what a fucking stupid useless thought, and I think, I'm glad at least it wasn't my father, and I think, Mark has those two little girls and a shudder runs the length of my body, and then it occurs to me to wonder if I have miscarried, and then to wonder how I could not have miscarried. I manage to pull down my pants and feel my panties and on the outside they are dry, I pull them down too and look, no spotting. I sit on the toilet and force myself to pee and look and there is no sign of blood. How can this be? How can a new life possibly continue to grow in the midst of this war zone?

I sat in my car while the engine warmed, while the heat came up, until the shaking in my hands subsided enough that I could fish my phone out of my bag and call my father's cell. Please pick up I said out loud, and then he did.

"Becky. Where are you?"

"Out in my car, Dad."

A pause, I could feel him trying to figure out why in the hell I would be calling from my car. "Just getting here?"

"Actually just leaving."

I tell him that I got sick right after I arrived, that I've been in the bathroom throwing up and now I have to get home.

"Another stomach bug?"

"Something like that."

"Are you okay to drive? Do you need me to take you?"

"No, I'll manage. Dad, what I need is for you to tell Mom. I'm in no condition to deal with her shit."

"Right," he said. "I understand."

Well. Wonder of fucking wonders, it all comes back to her now, the FB. It only took thirty years of stumbling around in the dark and now finally the lightbulb shines and what am I supposed to do, clap my hands? Feel sorry for her? You know, say Oh you poor thing, all is forgiven? Not on your fucking life.

This is the place where I live. This is the fucking dungeon. Makes her want to puke her guts out? Well try calling this home every day for thirty years. You think I've gotten used to it? You think I've stopped asking why this happened to me? You think I ever forget? I may be a little girl but I know what's what, I know SO much more than her even now that she's made her great discovery.

Here's what—life is being little and getting ripped into pieces and no one ever comes to help and there is fucking nothing you can do about it and it's your own fault anyway because all you are is a stupid little piece of shit. Welcome to the club, FB.

Eleven

These things happened that summer.

For six weeks Lathsamy called herself Lulu.

She believed she was being pursued by the CIA, that they had commandeered an apartment in the building across the street and were using a telescope to observe her. She boarded her windows with plywood. She said that Jeffrey was a psychiatrist who had been assigned by Beth Israel Hospital to keep tabs on her. She believed that someone was coming into her apartment and lacing the food with anti-psychotic medication. She told me all this.

There was a night, a week after she'd been in the hospital at Beth Israel, that started like other nights with Lulu pacing the apartment, but then as the hours passed she worked herself into a frenzy. She talked to herself, went through her litany of grievances; she swore, she said terrible things about Jeffrey, she slammed doors. Eventually she overturned chairs, threw papers and books on the floor. She took a razor blade to the Gohonzon, her Buddhist scroll, and slashed it into thin strips. She screamed at the Buddha. She smashed plates.

Jeffrey told me later that he tried once to intervene, tried twice, and each time Lathsamy (he would not call her Lulu) only escalated more. Then he went to check on Eddie, hoping that somehow the little boy was sleeping through this horror, and instead found him awake, trembling, in tears. As Jeffrey sat huddled with his son in the boy's room, behind a closed door, they heard the impact of something being thrown, the shattering of glass, which later proved to have been a large framed mirror in the hallway. More shattering, the bathroom mirror. Later he learned that after smashing the mirrors, Lathsamy walked back and forth, back and forth over the shards of glass, embedding many of them in her bare feet. Finally at 4 A.M. a neighbor called the police who came and had an ambulance take Lathsamy to the emergency room at Cambridge Hospital.

In the ER there was another evaluation, another decision to commit Lathsamy to a psychiatric unit. Again she needed to be medically cleared, her blood sugar was dangerously high; again she was admitted to a medical unit to have her diabetes stabilized before she would be sent to the psych unit. When Jeffrey called me in the morning he was distraught about the condition of his wife, also about his own lack of judgment in keeping Eddie at home that week, having convinced himself that the boy needed the stability of being with his parents and not shuffled back and forth to his grandparents, even if his mother was unwell. Jeffrey, crying, told me that he would never forgive himself for what he, a protective service worker, had exposed his son to, the trauma the boy had suffered. Still, he said, Lathsamy was where she needed to be, he was hopeful that she would finally receive treatment that could restore her sanity. So was I.

That evening Jeffrey called again, beside himself, saying he had just been informed by the hospital that Lathsamy had stabilized, medically and psychiatrically, and they were discharging her. He had asked to speak to the psychiatrist, told him that the exact same thing had happened at Beth Israel only a week before and she had not stabilized, she had only gotten worse. Didn't the doctor understand it was less than twenty-four hours since Lathsamy had been overturning furniture and screaming in the middle of the night, smashing mirrors and impaling her feet on broken glass? The doctor calmly told Jeffrey that because his wife had not signed a release, he could listen but could not discuss the case. Now Jeffrey was pleading with me to intervene. I told him that I could not overrule a doctor but I would call the hospital and try to speak to him. I did, and he told me the same thing, he would need the patient's consent to discuss anything with me and he did not have it. Later that evening, Lulu was sent home.

She showed up for every one of our appointments during the period when she was Lulu, and every Friday afternoon I was surprised when she walked in the door. But some thread of connection kept her coming back. There was an eerieness to her appearance, in her tank tops with no bra, her exposed belly button, the little skirts or short shorts and boots up to the tops of her calves, the heavy mascara and glaring lipstick and red cheeks. She was a caricature, grotesque and infinitely sad with her long trails of self-mutilation, but the eerie thing was how much she looked like a little girl dressed up as a sex worker. She had lost weight and her breasts looked barely formed, her hips shapeless. Was this how they had dressed her and made her up when she was twelve? She paced and talked, repeating the same complaints, disparaging the people who pretended to care for her, angry, terrified, rarely willing to listen to anything I tried to say. She spent portions of several sessions speaking a language I assumed at the time to be Lao, though months later she told me it was Thai, said that large swaths of Thai had come back to her when she was Lulu.

One time she brought something she had written to our session. It was like a nightmare version of the writing she'd shown me as Lathsamy. She had printed in block letters, sharp jutting lines in heavy black that showed through on the back of the paper and while she might have done this with marker, I wondered if she had brushed mascara onto the page.

MARRIAGE = CONCENTRATION CAMP
BANGKOK IS EVERYWHERE BANGKOK=BANG COCK
HITLER LIVES
HITLER LIVES IN ME I AM POISONED I AM TOXIC
I TURN MEDICINE INTO POISON

BANG YOUR COCK INTO ME BABY GIVE IT TO ME GIVE
IT TO ME

I DESERVE THIS LOOK AT ME LOOK AT THIS BODY IN
MY LAST LIFE I WAS A NAZI DOCTOR

AUSCHWITZ

I REMEMBER

I SIGNED DEATH WARRANTS

I EXAMINED BODIES I CALLED THEM FILTH VERMIN
NOW I AM FILTH VERMIN

NO COINCIDENCE I WAS CHOSEN

THERE ARE NO COINCIDENCES ONLY KARMA ONLY
POISON MY BODY IS FULL OF POISON THEY ARE ONTO
ME I AM ONTO THEM I SEE THROUGH EVEYONE I SEE
THROUGH EVERYTHING I AM ALL KNOWING BANG ME
BABY

BANG YOUR HOT JUICY COCK INTO ME BABY I DE-
SERVE THIS IT IS MY KARMA THEY ARE EVERYWHERE I
AM ONE OF THEM THEY ARE AGENTS OF THE UNIVERSE

THE UNIVERSE HAS ITS BIG JUICY BANGKOK UP MY
ASS

As I read Lulu stomped back and forth and when I looked up she
had stopped right in front of my chair and was glaring down at me.
She was hardly a large woman but in that moment, hovering above
me she seemed huge, not menacing to me but overpowering. I didn't
know what to say. As a therapist that's not a place you ever want to be
but that's where I was and naturally she picked right up on it. "Poor
Becky," she said, her voice cutting the air. "I frighten you, I scare you
speechless. Well who could blame you, a Nazi in your office, a Nazi
a Nazi a Nazi whore. Don't worry Becky you don't have to be scared
for me. I know what I'm doing I'm good at it I'm a pro and they are
idiots. They're not worth your little finger. I'll keep them away from
you I promise. I know just what to do. Please a man any man they
think they're fucking me but I have them eating out of my hand."

Then she was on the move again, back and forth, back and forth and finally it occurred to me to say that she was in Hell but weren't there still three thousand possibilities in every moment, but by then she wasn't listening.

At home things shifted after she was discharged from Cambridge Hospital. According to Jeffrey there was no more screaming at night, no more smashing of things. Instead she spent increasing amounts of time out of the apartment, always made up and dressed in those tight revealing outfits. The evening she got back from the hospital, when Jeffrey told her that Eddie was staying with his grandparents for a few days until things settled down, she tossed her head and said the boy who had been in the apartment was not her son, he could be on the moon for all she cared. She said to Jeffrey that she was going out to live her life. But she told me that she was being instructed by the traffickers to go to bars and pick up certain men and have sex with them, that they had her son and this was the price for keeping him alive.

Some nights she went out and didn't come home. It was more alarming than when she stayed in the apartment, where Jeffrey could be aware of what was happening, however bad, and at least we could know if she was physically safe. But in her condition, out in the world, at the mercy of who knew what or whom? Was she truly going to bars and picking up men? Truly having sex with them? Was she using condoms? Was she prostituting? She told me that the traffickers were communicating to her telepathically and men were making electronic payments, at least half of which was plainly delusional, but who could say what really was going on? Was she, as seemed unbearably likely, exposing herself to physical violence? Was she doing even the most basic self-care, eating, testing her blood sugar, giving herself insulin, taking her other medication? And at a still more basic level, what was happening to her as a human being? What could her days and nights possibly be other than a stream of chaos and terror?

One Friday she showed up at my office with a large bruise on her cheek which she had tried to cover with make up. She was not willing to talk about it but here was actual evidence that our fears were not exaggerated. One of the times she didn't return home, it turned out she spent the night and half the next day in the emergency room at Tufts Medical Center, after having screamed at a liquor store clerk and refused to leave the premises; in the ER, following what had become the established pattern, she eventually convinced the psychiatrist that she was stable and not dangerous, and she was released. The next week there was another known incident, she went home with a man and ended up throwing dishes at him; the police were called, she was taken to yet another emergency room, was again discharged without being hospitalized.

At the end of July, Lulu moved out of her apartment. She had been spending less and less time there, but this was different, a clear statement that to her the marriage was over. Jeffrey, despite everything, tried to convince her to wait until she was well before making a decision of such magnitude. She told him she was well, had never in her life been better. She went to stay with a woman named Ruth from her Buddhist group, after packing two suitcases and telling Jeffrey that everything else of hers should be burned. But three days later Ruth called Jeffrey and told him that Lathsamy had accused her of betraying her trust, something to the effect that Ruth was chanting in code and giving secrets away to the bugs planted in her home, and Lathsamy had taken her bags and stormed out.

On a dreadful day in early August I got a call from the Clerk's office at the Boston courthouse. Lathsamy had shown up there wearing a minidress with a plunging neckline, calling herself Lulu, claiming that other lawyers had stolen all her cases, demanding them back. In fact before her surgery Lathsamy had asked several of her colleagues to cover her cases until she recovered, and it was obvious that she was in no condition now to resume her practice. In the Clerk's office she started yelling, claimed the Court personnel were conspiring to prevent her from making a living. In the end two Court Officers forcibly escorted her from the building, each taking her by an arm while she accused them of assaulting her, threatened to bring suit, said they didn't know who they were dealing with. All this took place in that busy courthouse in front of people who had known and respected Lathsamy as a colleague, attorneys and social workers, one of the judges who happened to be walking down the corridor. In the Clerk's Office they found paperwork listing me as an emergency contact. The person who called me said everyone there was very concerned.

A few days later Lulu went off with a man to Ogunquit, Maine, a resort town on the coast. The police, whose report was summarized in hospital notes I eventually received, would later determine that she and the man had registered in a motel for two nights, Thursday and Friday. On Saturday morning they checked out. The man apparently then left Ogunquit. Lulu stayed. Using information they obtained from the motel, the police were able to reach the man by phone. He told them that Lulu had flipped out and refused to get in his car, so he left her. There was no evidence, according to the police, of anything illegal having happened. Lulu walked through Ogunquit, carrying her two suitcases, trying to find another motel. It was Saturday in the middle of August, the height of tourist season, and there were no rooms anywhere. Then she wandered up and down the one main street of the little town, finally stopped and parked herself on a sidewalk in front of a grocery store, sat on one of her bags, chanted, then tried to talk to people who passed by. One woman exchanged a few words with her and Lulu got up, started speaking rapidly, some of her words not in English. The woman walked away; Lulu followed her, and the woman, alarmed and frightened, called the police. When the police asked her if she was planning to hurt anyone, or hurt herself, Lulu told the officer that she was going to chant until someone killed her.

She was taken to the emergency room of the closest hospital in the nearby town of York. Another psychiatric evaluation. But this time she was in a plainly helpless state, alone in a strange place, grossly delusional, beyond the pale of what any psychiatrist could consider a condition suitable for discharge. She was admitted to a psychiatric unit at the Southern Maine Medical Center.

By this point I had been working with Lathsamy for over seven years. I can't begin to say what it's like to watch someone you love, someone you have seen blossoming against the longest odds, to watch her disintegrate, lose herself, overpowered by forces that once destroyed her childhood and had now returned to destroy her again. In my profession we have antiseptic terms for this, manic episode and dissociative identity disorder and traumatic reenactment syndrome, language that at the end of the day only serves as a shield against our true feelings. My true feelings.

There was a point in one of our sessions that summer, it might have been her calmest moment as Lulu, when she was sitting still, was almost reflective. She looked at me with narrowed eyes and said, "You think I'm psychotic, don't you?"

I wanted to say that I thought there was truth in her beliefs, but it was the truth of the years when she had been Lulu as a girl in Bangkok, not the current reality. But I knew if I said something like that she would only take it as an evasion or a lie. So instead I said, simply, "Yes."

She smirked, but tears began to trickle out of the corners of her eyes as she said in the voice of a little girl, "And I thought you believed in me."

Twelve

After a week the hospital in Maine discharged Lathsamy. While she was there she signed a release for the hospital staff to communicate with me. Her discharge paperwork described her as "a thirty-five year old Thai woman who claims to be a Harvard educated attorney." I found it disconcerting, to say the least, that they got her nationality wrong and implied that her statements about her profession and education were not credible. I had spoken to a social worker from her unit several times. I told her that Lathsamy was Laotian and confirmed that she was a Harvard graduate and had been a practicing attorney before her surgery. Maybe they didn't believe me either.

But my main complaint was that I felt they should have kept her longer. I didn't see how a week could possibly be long enough to bring her to a place of emotional safety from which she could start to put herself back together. I argued with them on the phone, the social worker, the doctor, to no avail. I was told they had started her on new medications, a mood stabilizer and an anti-psychotic, that she was complying, promised to keep taking them after she got out—and the new meds appeared to be effective. She was refusing to attend therapy groups on the unit. The social worker said they didn't believe there was anything else they could do for her.

At some point during her stay in the hospital she started responding when addressed as Lathsamy, and by the end of the week that's what she was calling herself again. She agreed to have Jeffrey pick her up. He drove the two hours to Biddeford, Maine and found his wife sedated, her speech halting and unclear, her thoughts fuzzy, her movements very slow. But she was willing to return to their apartment, was accepting his support, Jeffrey reported to me after they got home. She wasn't saying anything delusional. She seemed fragile to him but different, in a good sense, than she had been all summer. She had apologized for creating so much havoc. She described herself as having gone crazy. He told me that he still loved her, wanted her back, he hoped they could reconstruct their marriage.

But by the time she came to see me the next day, already she had deteriorated. Not in the manner of the previous two months, but in other ways which would set the direction for many of the events that followed. Lathsamy inched her way into my office, barely able to walk. Jeffrey had driven her, was sitting in the waiting area, there was no way she could have traveled by herself. One look and I knew she was suffering severe side effects from the new medication and I thought—how could they have released her from the hospital in this condition? Or even if she had not been like this when the decision was made, how could they not have kept her long enough to be sure she was tolerating the meds? I was appalled, outraged, but here she was and this was going to have to be dealt with. She was willing to start seeing her psychiatrist again, agreed to talk to her on the phone as soon as she could be reached, so her meds could be adjusted.

The sight of Lathsamy was heartbreaking and it was not just the extreme rigidity of her muscles, her impaired mobility, shocking as that was. She was dressed in jeans and a tee shirt, bone thin, her face sagging, her eyes dull and defeated, this woman whose eyes used to blaze, who had been so animated and energetic, her speech lively, her mind incisive. Even through the horrors of the past two months she had been on fire with rage. Now she seemed simply to have burned out. Yes, some of this was from being overmedicated, but not all, at least that was my gut response to seeing her. I thought—and I felt—that this was a broken woman.

* * *

Lathsamy was in no state of mind to reflect on her period as Lulu, the chaos of the past two months, the psychological impact of her surgery and before that her speech at the sex trafficking conference. She was confused and frightened by her physical state, as anyone would be. And once I had explained the side effects to her, told her slowly and carefully what could be done to help her, once we had put in the call to her psychiatrist, she lurched into a long lament about Eddie, about the wrong being done to her by Jeffrey.

She was recognizing Eddie as her son again. When she got home from the hospital Eddie wasn't there, of course not, she said: he was three years old and couldn't be left alone in the apartment. Jeffrey had told her that the boy was with his grandparents, and in the moment she made nothing of it, she took for granted that he would be coming home some time that day. It was only later, apparently after Jeffrey had spoken to me, and Eddie still not there, that she thought to ask when he would be home. Jeffrey told her that he would be sleeping at his grandparents' that night, he thought it best to give Lathsamy a chance to get settled. Tomorrow then? No, he had told her, not tomorrow either. How long? Only then did Jeffrey tell her he wanted to give it a month. Give it a month? she'd said. Give what a month? And Jeffrey said, a month before Eddie would come back to live in their apartment. Lathsamy asked why. Jeffrey said he wanted to make sure Eddie would not again be exposed to the things he had seen and heard that summer. What things, Lathsamy asked. Screaming, Jeffrey told her, and smashing mirrors, and Lathsamy coming and going and not being able to be a mother for her son. You mean me being a crazy woman, Lathsamy said. Jeffrey didn't answer. She asked him if he thought she was still crazy. He said they just needed time to make sure she was stable. So you're keeping my son from me for a month, she said. And he said yes.

Lathsamy recounted this to me slowly, painstakingly, with many pauses to collect herself, gather her words, to fight back tears, and finally she allowed herself to cry in small gasps. "I'm being punished for having a breakdown," she said. "Why does Jeffrey think I'm still crazy? Can't he tell the difference?...This is the stigma of mental illness....Suppose I had cancer. Suppose I was in the hospital for a week for treatment...What kind of husband would keep my son away from me? For a month?" Tears came slowly again, as if she lacked the physical capacity to cry harder. She glanced toward the window on her right, then down at her hands which were shaking in her lap and then back up at me. "You see how I am, Becky. After all I've been through...my own husband...he's taking my child away from me. I gave birth to that child....He lived inside my body....How can he do this to me?"

She spoke to me with a muted anger, the charred remains of the summer's rage. She had no perspective on how her behavior had affected Eddie, no psychic space to understand the child's needs, and it was not my job in that moment to try to tell her things I knew she couldn't hear and have her feel that I was siding with Jeffrey. My job was what it always had been, to be a safe person for her, to help her feel heard, to hold her and her pain. Still, I felt that I was watching her sink into a kind of permanent defeat, a resignation that she would always be the victim, as if in some deep place she knew that her struggles had been waged and lost, and she could never escape her history.

Thirteen

When I was eight years old, I would get out of school about an hour before my mother got out of work. Sometimes I would make a plan ahead of time to go over to a friend's house and sometimes I would come home. I liked this, it made me feel trusted and grown up. I had my own key to the back door. My brother was never home, he was out doing whatever it was that fifteen year old boys did, and I would have the house to myself until Mom came in. Sometimes I would play records or watch TV, sometimes I would read or start my homework, and sometimes, if Mom had told me what we'd be having for dinner I would get it started with the things I knew how to do, just to have a nice surprise for her.

My brother was never there except for one day when he was. I had gone up to my room and I didn't know he was in the house. I loved my room with its glistening hardwood floor; when I was younger I used to believe the wood had come from a tree that shined like that until my dad explained to me that it was because of something called polyurethane that got brushed onto the boards, and after that I felt like I was old and knowing, but still sometimes I would get down onto the floor and run my hand along the wood in a place where a knot showed and pretend I was in the forest touching a live tree. I had my own cassette player, and a cabinet with glass doors where I kept my tapes. Even though it was easy I was proud of myself when I pushed the right buttons to make the cassette player do what I wanted; I like the whirring sound it made when I selected rewind or fast forward, and I imagined tiny mice scampering inside the machine. More than anything else I loved my bedspread which first had been my Grandma Millie's and then my mother's when she was a girl and then passed down to me. It was all faded so the colors were extra soft and delicate, mainly pastels, green and yellow and blue and pink, with a smattering of white. The spread was laid out in squares and most of the squares were small but every so often there was one that was quadruple the size and had three blue flowers side by side with yellow centers and green stems with leaves hanging like double sets of arms off each stem. Another of the big squares had a pink outside border and inside that a green border with blue dots, and inside that a branch bending down with green leaves and blue blossoms, and some of the smaller squares were solid colors and some had little patterns. The cotton was soft from all its years of use and I liked to bury my face in it and close my eyes and imagine my grandmother as a little girl lying on this very same spread.

That afternoon I was on my bed on my stomach, propped up on my elbows, I'd left my door open so I'd be able to hear Mom when she came in and I was just going to start my homework, it was multiplication problems, and suddenly there was my brother in the doorway. "Hi there Becky," he said and he had this goofy grin on his face and he was holding a 16 ounce bottle of Coke in his right hand.

"Hi Mark," I said, and it felt strange that he was home and even stranger that he was seeking me out, which he never did, but I didn't give it that much thought.

"Want to have some fun?"

"Sure," I said and I put my pencil down.

He came in and I sat up on the bed and he offered me some Coke and I said thanks. He handed me the bottle and I took a sip and it tasted strange and it burned my throat and it felt warm on my insides and he said it was Happy Coke. I asked him why it was Happy Coke and he said because it makes you happy. He grabbed the bottle and took a big drink from it and he grinned even more and handed it back to me and said I should have some more. So I took another sip and the same thing happened, I felt even warmer inside and he said have some more so I did and he asked if I liked it and I said yes and he asked if it was making me happy and I said yes it was.

Then he took the bottle and drank from it, and we passed it back and forth, and I was getting dizzy and nothing on my wall would hold still and I started to laugh and then we both were laughing, he burped and then I burped and we laughed some more. He put his arm around my shoulders and he said "Becky, you're my sweetheart," I thought it was the silliest thing and I laughed and laughed. He asked if I wanted to play a game and I said sure. He said he would ask me questions and if I got the answers right, for each time I was right he would take off a piece of his clothing and if I got the answer wrong I would take off a piece of my clothing but he was sure that wouldn't happen because I was such a smart little girl.

"Okay sweetheart?" he said and I said okay. He asked me what was the tallest mountain in the world and I said Mount Everest and he laughed and said, "I told you you were smart," and he took off his shirt and underneath the blue button down shirt he was wearing a white tee-shirt. He asked me how much was four times seven and that was easy because we were learning the multiplication table and I said twenty-eight and he took off his tee-shirt. He kept asking me easy questions and I kept knowing the answers and I really liked the game, I liked being smart and even though things were spinning I could see that he was taking off his shoes and then his socks, one and then the next and then his belt and then he took off his green pants.

His underpants were white and they ended down below his belly button and I had never seen a boy's undies before and his big penis, I knew that's what it was called and I had never seen one but I knew what it was for, I knew that's what boys used to pee and what a man used with a woman to make a baby. It was right there, I could see the shape of it and I couldn't believe how big it was, and I thought, how can he walk around with that all day, how can he even lie down to go to sleep at night? Mark could see that I was staring at it and he said "You want to see it, don't you" and I didn't say anything, even all happy and dizzy, like I knew it wasn't right. He said that for a bonus because I was so smart and such a sweetheart and I got all the other questions right, he would take off his underpants without me even having to get one more question right, "You'd like that wouldn't you, sweetheart," he said, and I didn't answer and he slid off his underpants and there it was. There it was and I was shocked by all the ugly black hair above it; I had no idea boys were hairy like that and below the hair his penis was sticking straight out and there was a funny shape like a bulb at the end of it, and I thought that's where he pees from and I thought wouldn't it be funny if he started to pee now and I was laughing, and he stood up and faced me and he was laughing, and I thought oh no he's going to pee on me, but instead he said, "Come on sweetheart let's dance." He grabbed my hand and pulled me off the bed and I was standing in front of him and he was swaying in front of me; I thought if we're dancing I should put on a tape, but the room was spinning behind him and all around him and the next thing I knew I was on my butt on the floor.

After that what I remembered were the same things that happened in my dream, his big body next to me on the floor, the iron grip of his hand below my shoulder, the odor of bourbon, the reek of his sweat, his voice booming into my ear, me being crushed under his heavy weight, his tongue jamming into my little mouth and then his hand over it and not being able to breathe and all the things he kept telling me about what I wanted him to do. Except I also remembered other things. I remembered the way he kept ramming his penis into me and it would go a little deeper each time, three four five six times and the way he grunted with each hammer blow and the sheer raw pain of being torn open and the feel of my body being ripped apart and knowing that I was going to die. I remembered the feel of it when some last piece of something came loose, the feel of it as that whole huge penis came down into me, I knew the size of it and now it was in my body and it was something impossible, it was something more terrifying even than the pain, even than the certainty of my own death, it was a wrongness so vast and so nameless and so completely outside of anything I had ever known or ever imagined that all I could do was to find some way to not feel it, to not know it.

That was when I found out I had a switch. It was a simple, ordinary switch, on and off, like any switch you use to turn a light on, to turn a light off. I pushed the switch and turned everything off. It was ridiculous, how easy it was.

The next thing I remembered was him standing up and I was still lying on my back on the floor. I looked up at him and he was like a giant but his penis wasn't as big and I thought that's weird, and he looked down still grinning but then his face changed and he said, "Oh shit! Look what you've done." I didn't know what he meant, and he pulled on his clothes and raced out of the room and he came back with a sponge in one hand and tissues in the other and he said, "Get up." I tried and I couldn't, he threw the sponge and the tissues down and he stuck his hands in my armpits and jerked me up and then I saw the blood on the floor and I still wasn't feeling anything, he bent down for the tissues and handed me some and said, "For fuck's sake, wipe yourself up." He used the sponge to clean the blood off the boards, which got shiny again as the sponge sucked the blood off of them. I reached down and wiped myself with the tissues and I thought the bleeding wouldn't stop but it did. I didn't know what to do with the tissues and he grabbed them from me and left the room and then I heard the toilet flush, and I was just standing there wobbly on my feet and he came back and picked up my panties from the floor and told me to put them on so I did. Then he handed me peppermints to eat, one after the other, he told me to eat them so Mom wouldn't know when she got home. He said it was a really bad thing I'd done, drinking bourbon and I was only a little girl and if Mom found out I would get in more trouble than I could possibly imagine. He said if Mom ever found out what he and I had done together I would get in even more trouble than that, they would probably send me away, Mom and Dad. Something happened then inside me, I didn't mean to push the switch but I must have because I was feeling so scared, and I was crying. He told me I better stop crying or he would smack me so hard that I would really have something to cry about, was that what I wanted, and I said no and I stopped myself from crying and he gave me another peppermint. Then he went away and I lay down on the bed and I fell asleep.

When I woke up Mom was home and sitting next to me on the bed. She asked if I was all right and I said I was sick which was true and I went to the bathroom and threw up.

* * *

So many details came back from that first time, the ugly olive green of his pants, the loose thread hanging from the little button that held down one side of the collar of his powder blue short sleeved Oxford shirt, the cut on the right side of his upper lip, how it was scabbed over and angled up toward his nostril. The texture of the skin on his fingers, strangely smooth and soft like the skin of a little boy.

The second time was a distinct memory, too. Another day after school, not right away, maybe a week had passed or a few weeks; the passage of time was fuzzy but what happened was clear. I got home from school and there he was, waiting for me in the back hall when I walked in the door. He was holding a bottle of Coke, 16 ounces. He was grinning. Looking back, I could have turned around and walked right out the door, but in that moment it never crossed my mind.

"Hi there Becky," he said.

"Hi," I said. I closed the door behind me. To the right of the door there were hooks on the wall to hang coats, there was a mat for shoes, to the left were the stairs to the basement and straight ahead was the kitchen. That's where he was, right where the kitchen ended and the little hall began, he was big and he was swinging the Coke bottle slowly back and forth and he said, "Want to get happy again?"

"I don't know," I said.

"You liked Happy Coke, you know you did. That's what you told me, Becky, how much you liked it, didn't you?"

"Yes."

"You weren't lying to me, were you?"

"No."

"Besides," Mark said, "I have something special planned for you."

"What?"

"You have to come upstairs to find out. But it's something you'll like. I promise."

I liked special things and he was promising and I wanted so much to believe him. I took off my jacket and hung it up on a hook that I could reach, and I took off my shoes and left them on the mat. We went upstairs and Mark said we should go into my room so we did and he closed the door. He opened the bottle of Coke and handed it to me and said I should have some so I took a sip and it burned going down and he took the bottle and he drank from it and he gave it back to me and I took another sip. We were just standing there in the middle of my room and I was starting to feel warm inside again and he said, "Now doesn't that feel good? Doesn't that make my little sweetheart feel happy?" He was wearing a blue sweatshirt that said University of Michigan in gold letters on the front and facing him my line of vision came to the middle of the sweatshirt right where the Michigan was and I thought, we live in Massachusetts, why doesn't it say Massachusetts?

But I didn't ask about the name of the state on his sweatshirt, I looked up at his face and it was all goofy again and I could see hairs on the inside of his nostrils and that made me feel goofy, so I laughed and I said it felt good. He grabbed the bottle and took another drink and he said he felt good too, and he said why don't we sit down so we did on my bed.

After we sat down and I drank some more Happy Coke and he

drank some more he said, "Does my sweetheart want to know what her special thing is?"

Of course I wanted to know and he said, "I'm going to let you give me a whipping."

"A whipping?" I said, and he said, "Don't you think I deserve to be whipped? Don't you think I was a naughty boy before? Wasn't I naughty to my little sweetheart?"

I didn't know what to say so I didn't say anything and he said, "Of course that's what you think," and he made a big burp and he laughed and I laughed. "Of course you want to give me a whipping. And I want you to give me a whipping because I deserve it. Okay? Say okay, sweetheart."

So I said okay. I was feeling warm and happy and dizzy, and he wanted me to give him a whipping, and it was my special thing.

He told me I was going to whip his bare bottom. He told me I was going to use his belt. He told me I was his sweetheart. He told me I could whip him for as long as I felt like. He told me again he wanted me to do this. He said he wouldn't do anything to hurt me back. "That's a promise," he said. "You have my word. You believe me, don't you, sweetheart?"

I said I believed him, and I really did.

He pulled off his pants. He stood up and shook his belt loose from his pants, and his pants dropped to the floor. He handed me the belt and he said to get up and I did. He pulled down his undies and stepped out of them and there was his gigantic penis again, sticking straight out. He got on the floor face down and I couldn't understand how he could be lying right on top of his penis but he was, and he turned his face to the side so he could talk and he said, "Now go ahead, sweetheart, whip me. Go ahead and whip me."

I was shaky on my feet and I was dizzy but I knew I needed to do this. I kept the buckle end of the belt in my hand, I pulled my arm back and aimed the other end of the belt at his bare butt and I hit it, and he said, "Harder." So I did it again but harder this time, and he said "That's it, now even harder" and I kept whipping his butt with the belt and he kept saying harder and I kept swinging it harder until I was using all my might and I couldn't do it any harder. I was getting all sweaty and his butt was getting all red and he was right, it was special and it was fun and I liked being the one with the belt in my hand, I really liked him being down there on the floor and me being above him, I knew I was hurting him and I liked that too and besides it was what he wanted so that made it okay. I kept swinging and swinging the belt and I was laughing and I was having fun until all of a sudden he roared "YOU LITTLE FUCKING BITCH" and he bolted up and he yanked the belt from my hand, I was sure he was going to whip me but instead he threw the belt across the room, hard, the buckle clanged when it hit my bureau and his face was red and his penis was right there. I didn't know what he was going to do and then he grabbed my shoulders and pushed me down hard onto the floor and he put his body on top of me, his hand was over my mouth and I couldn't breathe and with his other hand he pushed my skirt up and pulled my panties down, I knew what he was going to do and before he could start ramming his penis into me I pulled the switch and I didn't feel a thing.

After he got off me I was sure I must have bled again but I hadn't. He gave me peppermints to eat just like the last time and made me promise not to tell Mom and he said again how much trouble I would get in if I told, and he left and I got into my bed and I feel asleep, and when I woke up Mom was home and I was sick.

* * *

After that, my memories blurred together. The same basic script played out over and over again. We're alone in the house together. Mark lures me with alcohol and promises. He tells me what he will let me do to him, what he will not do to me. He makes it fun, he makes it enticing, he makes it a chance to do something forbidden. He preys on my desire to get him back for everything he has done to me. I always believe him. I never say no. He always loosens me with the alcohol. He always lets me do to him whatever it was he promised, always something that inflicts real physical pain. I'm always happy to hurt him. I always think that this time he's keeping his word. At the critical moment he always turns on me. I always turn off my feelings before he can ram his penis into me. He always makes me feel I have done something so horrible that I would never dare to tell. At the end I sleep. When I wake up, usually I'm sick. And then I go on with my little girl life as if nothing has happened.

I don't know how many times he raped me, but I know it was a lot, I can feel this with certainty in my body. At some point he stopped. I never knew why. And then I forgot about it.

Fourteen

I referred Lathsamy and Jeffrey to a marriage counselor. At the same time the psychiatrist changed Lathsamy's medication and she gradually regained her mobility, though she developed a facial twitch, another side effect which would persist for more than a year. A month passed and she remained subdued, slept at night, did not have outbursts, did not go out to bars to pick up men, showed no signs of psychosis. In short she was Lathsamy and not Lulu, and as Lathsamy she settled into a kind of depression. But I don't think she was back to any version of her old self. This was new territory, a life being lived in a quietly desperate place where she had lost belief in herself and her connection to the world.

She went to the counseling sessions with Jeffrey for months and I believe that both of them really did try to work things out. But they never could find a common language, a way to understand together so much that had come unglued and how it could be repaired. At least that was what I gathered from Lathsamy's accounts. She felt constantly judged and under attack, blamed for things beyond her control, held to an impossible standard as a spouse and parent, disparaged for an illness she had never chosen. It was as if, for her, she had been pushed off the deck of a boat into high seas, was using every bit of strength she had to stay afloat, and she was being expected to take care of people sitting dry and safe on deck. It was impossible. Jeffrey complained, she said, that she was the one who had insisted on moving out and fracturing the marriage; it was an accusation, not only the words but the way he looked at her, the bitterness in his voice. Didn't he understand that she had been out of her mind? And on top of everything else, and also beneath it, were the issues to do with Eddie, his needs and his care, who came first and who had the right to determine what was best for whom, and the endless sting of being looked at as an unfit mother. Lathsamy never got over the hurt of having had Eddie kept away from her for a month, which in her heart had become a primal insult, this notion that her child needed to be protected from her.

After the first month passed, Eddie did return to live with Lathsamy and Jeffrey. But Lathsamy told me that she felt like a spectator witnessing the boy's life. Jeffrey hovered over everything to do with Eddie, got him up in the morning and fixed his breakfast, took him to pre-school and fetched him at the end of the day, attended to his care from dinner through bedtime, scheduled his play dates on weekends and took him to the park, to the Children's Museum. "I know I'm not well," Lathsamy said. "I can't do all the things Jeffrey does. I don't have the energy. I don't have the attention. But that isn't the point. The point is that I'm an outsider in my own home." She could feel Jeffrey day by day making Eddie his own territory, crowding her out, viewing each thing she was not doing for her son as more proof that she was not capable of being a mother, making it more and more impossible for her ever to become a real mother again, as if one stone after another were being added to an already crushing weight. "He has no faith in me. How can I have any faith in myself?"

But the worst thing, she said, was how Eddie accepted the situation. He seemed now to take for granted that she was not the one caring for him. "If he's hungry he goes to his father. If he's bored he goes to his father. He has a bad dream at night and calls for Daddy." He had learned to be polite to Lathsamy, to say hi with a forced little smile and go on with his day. He didn't complain about her spending so much time in bed or watching TV. He didn't seek her attention. "I wish," she said, "that he did demand my attention. I wish he would be upset with me. Angry with me. It would be better. It would mean I still have a place in his life. It would mean I'm being a bad mother. But I would still be a mother, Becky. Now I'm not any kind of mother at all."

Three months out of the hospital, she decided that she should go back to work. It was at least one thing she could do to contribute to her family, they certainly could use the money and she was also aware that the long unstructured days were only making things worse for her, reinforcing her feelings of being helpless and useless, and drawing her back into her familiar patterns of self-injury.

Back to work, that was what Lathsamy wanted, but not the work she had been doing before. She remembered going to the courthouse in the summer and making that huge scene, embarrassing herself in front of colleagues and the court personnel, and the shame of it made returning to that court unimaginable. Briefly she considered doing care and protection work in a different jurisdiction: it could be a fresh start with attorneys and social workers, court clerks and judges who didn't know her, who had no inkling of past events. But the thought of being a care and protection attorney again was salt in an open wound. How could she, whose own husband believed he needed to protect their son from her, how could she go out into the world and act as though she had the standing to protect other people's children? It would be a masquerade, she told me. Worse still, and this I think was the heart of the matter, was her fear that she herself could end up being accused of abuse or neglect, not just by implication or innuendo as she was now by her husband, but formally taken to court—and end up with custody removed from her by a judge. The image of it, a care and protection attorney being held up to public scorn and humiliation in her own field, how could she possibly subject herself to that?

So she began to talk about changing her area of practice. She spoke of immigration law, mobilized herself to do online research, and concluded that it was too complex for her to handle in her condition. Then she thought about becoming a defense attorney, perhaps a public defender. The areas she considered at this point were ones that could hold meaning for her, maybe not as much as care and protection once had, but still she could relate them to her own experience, the plight of immigrants and the indigent. But when she pictured herself back in the courtroom, in adversarial proceedings, the pressure and the volume of cases and the kinds of people she would have to deal with, and when she compared this with her life now, the days when she could barely get out of bed, she could see that this also would be too much.

Her next thought was wills and estates. Lathsamy believed she could handle the legal aspects. Most of the work would be outside of court, meeting with clients to help them draft or understand documents, walking them through legal procedures. Time in court would likely be routine, rarely adversarial, mainly a matter of managing the probate process. Maybe she could get something part time with a firm. Not especially meaningful, she said, but she had to be practical, this was what she was capable of, and she still would be providing a needed service.

She found a workshop for attorneys wanting to change their areas of practice. She went to it feeling, if not hopeful, at least determined. But she left at the first break. "It was impossible," she told me. "My hand shook taking notes. I couldn't concentrate. I couldn't retain information." I thought of Lathsamy during her years at Harvard, excelling in the most pressured, the most competitive possible classrooms at a time when she was in personal crisis. The distance she has traveled since then, I thought—so much lost and this terrible diminishing of her capabilities—how could she not have been thinking, been feeling the same thing about herself? "Imagine me sitting with clients," she said. "Imagine me standing before a judge, Becky. I can't do it."

After that, she decided to apply for Disability.

* * *

Social Security Disability Income, or SSDI, is a program for people with a medical condition, physical or mental, that prevents them from working. Lathsamy met the technical requirements: she'd worked enough years to qualify, and she had a clinical assessment of a psychiatric disability. She was plainly unable to work. Her psychiatrist supported her application and provided medical documentation. The only question was how long it would take for the Social Security bureaucracy to process and approve her claim, likely at least several months.

It was hard to tell what applying for Disability really meant to Lathsamy, how much it was a practical decision based on the reality of her condition, a kind of coming to grips, and how much she was simply giving up. At the time she talked about it as a way to contribute to her family and it was true that they were stretched thin on Jeffrey's salary as a protective services worker; what she was saying was perfectly valid as far as it went. But I wondered how far it did go. She had lost so much by then: the loving connection with her husband, her role as an active mother, a great deal of her ability to function, her sense of wholeness and coherence as a person, the glowing years of progress in recovery, the right to be viewed by others and by herself as normal rather than as someone mired in mental illness, and all this on top of the devastations of her childhood. And now a public statement of incapacity to fulfill a basic role of adulthood, earning a living. How could it not feel to her like an admission of failure?

When her SSDI came through it was almost summer again, and by then going on Disability turned out to mean something else, the option to separate from Jeffrey. Their marriage was in shambles, had been in shambles since Lathsamy crashed from her manic summer. What Jeffrey really wanted, she told me, was for her to be the person he thought he married, the brilliant incisive woman who had surmounted an unspeakable past, the heroic woman who had emerged from ashes and embodied the best of humanity. It was impossible, she said, she had never been that woman, she had been a time bomb.

She could never have truly stepped out of her history, and anyway, whatever self she had once been, she was not that woman now. All Jeffrey could see was what she was not, and the self she now was he kept fending off, fending off. What she wanted from Jeffrey was to be seen as someone who was seriously ill, who needed to be nursed back to health, but all his love was going to Eddie. She lamented that the child got his attention, his energy, always the child, and that she in her ragged useless state was only a burden. There was no sexual attraction between them, barely a friendship, hardly a hint of kindness. Most nights Jeffrey slept on the couch.

Lathsamy told me she had never thought of separation until she got the notification of her approval for SSDI, and I believe that was true. With the notice came a check for almost ten thousand dollars, a retroactive payment based on the date she was determined to have become disabled. Monthly payments were to start in July. It was only once she had the means to get out, literally held it in her hand, that she became aware of how trapped she had been feeling. Moving out had become a tangible possibility; it quickly became an irresistible force.

Irresistible, yes, but not impulsive, nothing like the separation of the previous summer, when she was Lulu, psychotic, agitated, barely able to see more than minutes or hours ahead, racing headlong into chaotic self-destruction. Lathsamy had tried to put her marriage back together, she had done what she was able, and it hadn't worked. She was suffocating. She had reason to feel unloved. She was confronted every day by her inability to function as a spouse and mother. In the face of this she wasn't flying out the door, wasn't making wild accusations. She was making a plan. She mobilized herself to look for an apartment, went on line to search listings, made phone calls, kept appointments. It was actually the most organized and functional she had been since her surgery.

Eventually she found a studio in a Dorchester neighborhood with a large Southeast Asian population. Her retroactive payment enabled her to put down the security deposit and first month, and to furnish the apartment. The rent would eat up a large portion of her monthly Disability check. But she still had several thousand dollars from the retro money as a cushion, she expected to get alimony and she vowed to be frugal.

On the first of August, Lathsamy moved. She felt what most of us would feel under similar circumstances, sad and scared but also a sense of emerging from despair. For first time in more than a year I heard her speak the word hope. She talked to me about her wedding day, about her expectations, her losses, her anger at Jeffrey, her sense of betrayal, her own shame. But she also was able to reflect on where she had been a year before, the disintegration of her life during that terrible summer; and she expressed feelings of accomplishment at having put herself back together as much as she had.

When I look back now, less than three years since she moved to Dorchester, knowing what I do, it's easy to feel foolish for having shared Lathsamy's hopefulness. But I did share it. She'd stayed out of the hospital, she was sane, she had survived the unraveling of her marriage and was making a new start.

There she is going on and on about What's Her Name, still, can you believe it? Well I believe it and I know why, I'm so wise that I know all the whys haha. I can tell you the reason for every single thing she does and doesn't do for whatever that's worth which is fucking nothing.

She thinks that talking about What's Her Name will get her out of her own mess. You might wonder what kind of sense that makes and I can tell you that too, it doesn't make any fucking sense. Anyway it's not the real reason, that's just her making believe which I always thought adults weren't supposed to do but that's the FB for you and the real reason? It's so she doesn't have to think about her own pathetic life.

Hope? Give me a fucking break.

I don't even know why I'm saying all this shit, it doesn't do anything for anyone and the joke is on me for even paying attention to what she says or doesn't say, thinks or doesn't think, who cares. You know what I am? A pathetic little bitch chasing my own fucking tail, I should call myself the plb, and what do you suppose I'll do with my tail if I ever catch it? Give it a good chomp, that's what.

Fifteen

November 25

BECKY CLIENT: The worst thing is that I never did a single fucking thing to try to stop him, I never said no, I always fucking believed him, I was the biggest stupid idiot in the fucking world. The first time okay but the second time I could have turned around and walked out the door, I mean there I was and there he was and he has that shit eating grin and I knew that grin, I knew perfectly fucking well what it was and what it meant and the fucking bottle of Coke and I stand there and I listen to him and his pathetic bullshit about something special for me, a fucking two year old could have seen through that, something special all right! And not just that time, I believed him every single fucking time, every time I let myself be sucked in, every time I drank the fucking Happy Coke, I let myself be turned into an eight year old lush and every single time I convinced myself it was going to be different, every time I was sure he wasn't going to do anything to me, and how

133

much smarts would it really have taken to put two and two together and come up with fucking four? What the fuck was wrong with me? You know, all I had to do was not come home after school. Once it started all I had to do was go over to one of my friends' house every day, or even if I didn't have that many friends or they got tired of me or whatever I could still have told Mom that I was going to someone's house and she would never have known and I could have walked around for an hour or gone to the library and I could have kept myself safe. Instead of doing what I did, which was to keep acting like it wasn't happening and it could never possibly happen again, instead of what I did which was to be complicit in my own fucking getting raped and not just once or twice but over and over and fucking over again.

BECKY THERAPIST: So you blame yourself for being fooled by your brother over and over again, every time you believed him and now it makes you feel like you were complicit.

BC: Yes! And it's not just a feeling, I WAS fucking complicit!

BT: But Becky, the truth is that you were eight and he was fifteen and he completely overpowered you, not just physically but psychologically. He manipulated you and he was really good at it, and it wasn't your fault that you believed him.

BC: Do NOT fucking patronize me! Don't you dare tell me what the truth is and what was or wasn't my fault! I know how old I was and how old he was and what he was good at and it doesn't mean shit! I could have said no, I could have turned around and walked out the fucking door, I could have said ~~Happy~~ Coke is a bunch of shit, and I could have said Mark don't take me for an idiot, I could have said go fuck yourself and I didn't do any of those things and don't you dare make excuses for me or try to say that it's all right when it was as not all right as anything in this fucking world could possibly be.

BT: So it's really important to you to take responsibility for your own choices, to recognize and own the things you could have done and didn't do, and it sounds like you're furious that I was trying to make excuses for you.

BC: Don't you see that it's the one thing I could have done for myself? Even if he had found other ways to rape me, I mean I know he was twice my size and I know if he got me alone with him he could do whatever he fucking wanted to my body, but I didn't have to let him touch my spirit. Can't you see that? Can't you see that he didn't just rape my body, he raped my spirit and I could have stopped him from raping my spirit and I didn't?

BT: There were two kinds of rapes that happened, what he did to your body and what he did to your spirit. And of the two, the rape of your spirit was the worst thing, because you could have had control over that, you could have stopped him from raping your spirit by standing up for yourself and saying no, and you never did that.

BC: Right. Exactly fucking right.

BT: Is there more...

BC: Of course there is fucking more! I just remembered

being repeatedly raped by my brother when I was eight years old and you're asking if there is more?...okay so the other worst thing is that he made me into a little fucking sadist, all that stuff with whipping him, inflicting pain and it's like he knew that the worst thing he could do to me was to make me be like him. You want to talk about truth, here is the fucking truth, I loved holding that belt and standing over him and whipping the shit out of him, I loved inflicting pain on his big ugly disgusting body, why do you think he could suck me in every time, it wasn't just the alcohol I mean yes I was into the fucking Happy Cokes and yes he could use that to lure me, and yes I believed him about promising not to hurt me, all that stuff I was saying just now is totally true. But it was this other thing, the completely shameful horrible thing was that he could lure me because I knew I would get to hurt him and there was nothing I wanted more in the world than to cause him pain. And don't go saying it was understandable that I would want to hurt him after what he did to me, I know it's fucking understandable and that doesn't make it all right and it doesn't change what he did to me, it doesn't change what I became, it's like he planted this shit seed inside me and watered it and then it just fucking blossomed and I became this fiend, I became this little fucking monster, I became someone who is no better than him, I became someone who took pleasure from inflicting pain, that is the fucking truth.

Wednesday morning. I called Mark's cell. A few rings and it went into fucking voicemail and I threw the phone down. I pace my apartment, too agitated to do anything else. A long hallway runs between my living room and kitchen, its walls are lined with photos of sand beaches on the Cape, rocky Maine coastlines, my favorite is one I took years ago from the peak of Mount Katahdin looking down on a cloud bank and usually when I walk down the hall it catches my eye but not today, I stride back and forth, back and forth and the walls barely exist, the doorway to the kitchen, the gray squares of linoleum on the other side, four chairs around a modest wooden table, pans hanging from a pegboard on the far wall, these things register in my brain in some useless way when I approach that end of the hall, they don't matter, all that matters is inside me, this boiling energy. I'm being just like Lathsamy during that horrible summer when she couldn't sit still—and so what if I am, I have the best fucking reasons in the world. At the other end I jut into the living room and grab the phone from where it landed on the couch and punch redial, and this time he picks up.

"Becky. What the hell happened to you last night?"

"I want you to get the fuck out."

"Whoa. What the fuck is going on here?"

If this is going to be a who-can-say-fuck-most contest I am going to fucking win. My hand is shaking on the phone, I have to use my other hand to steady it.

"Take your family and leave our house, Mark."

"Ah, it's our house, is it? Well if it's our house I have as much right to it as you do, don't I?"

"Don't fuck with me, Mark."

"Fuck with you? Who exactly is fucking with whom here? I have to say this is one of the more bizarre conversations I have had the misfortune of stumbling into. Would you like to tell me exactly what is going on?"

He knows. He's trying to sound casual, or is it ironic, or is it aggressive, the accomplished courtroom attorney toying with the opposing side. Whatever, I don't give a fuck. "You know what's going on."

"No, truly, I don't. But I'm beginning to believe that you need professional help."

"Fuck you Mark."

"All right Becky, enough. This is not only tiresome, it's also offensive. Either tell me what's behind your little temper tantrum or I'm going to hang up."

"You raped me, repeatedly, when I was eight years old. You want to talk to me about who's being fucking offensive?"

There was just the slightest pause. Then: "Well now, that is one creative fantasy."

"You wish."

"And to what do I owe the pleasure of being slapped in the face with this groundless accusation the morning before Thanksgiving?"

"I was sitting with your daughter last night when you came in the room and called her sweetheart. Sweetheart, that's what you would call me before you fucked me. Ring a bell, Mark?"

"Aha. I do believe I'm beginning to understand. This is one of those—what do you call it? Reconstituted memories?"

"Recovered memories is what you fucking call it."

"Right, recovered memories. Therapist speak for creative fantasies and groundless accusations. I've heard how this goes, where a therapist puts the idea into the deluded patient's head and voilà, a memory is born. Must be your bread and butter. And now, my goodness, here you are on the other end. Seeing a therapist yourself, are you?"

I listen to him and just feel myself deflating. I drop into the nearest chair, nothing left in my legs. Nothing left period. No more words. What did I think I was going to accomplish with this fucking phone call? Did I really believe he would admit to it? Or better yet apologize? Or say of course, Becky, whatever you want Becky, I'll clear out? I couldn't see beyond my own need to speak the truth to him, didn't have the smarts to wonder what this could possibly do for me, and at what cost. Now I find myself in tears and it is so fucking obvious that he will deflect anything I say, it should have been obvious before I ever picked up the phone if I weren't such a fucking idiot; and here I am thirty years later and he has me where he wants me one more time, him on top, him always on fucking top.

I know I should hang up, but before I can get my hand to move he pounces into the silence I have left for him and says, "Now listen to me Becky. It's time to be a grown up. If you ever say a word of this obscene lie to anyone, I will destroy you."

And I hear a voice come out of my mouth that I do not recognize as my own, and the voice says, "Mark, there is nothing you can do to me that you haven't already done."

When I called my father, he said, "Becky, are you all right?"

I said, "Dad, I am as not all right as you can possibly imagine. I need you and Mom to come over here so I can talk to you."

"When?"

"Now."

No fucking comment. I have nothing nothing nothing nothing nothing to say. I shouldn't even have a tongue. I'm going to lock my mouth and swallow the fucking key.

Sixteen

When I was ten, my family took a trip to New York City. We did the usual tourist things, saw The Phantom of the Opera, took a horse and carriage ride, went to the top of the Empire State Building, had dinner at a fancy French restaurant.

At one point on the second day Mark, who was seventeen, said he wanted to go do stuff by himself. My parents agreed and my mother said cheerfully, "Why don't you take Rebecca with you?"

The only thing I could think was how cool it would be to go off in the big city without my parents. I was having a good time and I wasn't minding being with Mom and Dad, but I just loved the idea that I was big enough and responsible enough to be sent unsupervised with my brother. "Yeah Mark," I said earnestly. "Why don't you take me with you?" He hesitated and I added, "Say yes, please."

And then he did say yes.

The abuse must have stopped by then. But it couldn't have been much more than a year and it might have been less than that. Still, enough time for me to have forgotten everything. It seems impossible, I know, but it's true.

So off we went. It was a warm day, humid the way New York gets in the summer, and we strolled lazily through Central Park. I wasn't the least bit apprehensive. Just the opposite, I felt thrilled. We didn't talk much which was fine with me, I hadn't gone off to have a conversation with my brother. I'd gone off to have an adventure in the city, something I could go home and tell my friends about. Mark had money and he offered to rent us a rowboat to go out on the Lake. I thought it was very nice of him.

There were so many things he could have done to me that afternoon. He could have lured me into a secluded spot in the park, I would have followed him anywhere. He could have had alcohol in his pocket. He could have done whatever he wanted to my body. He could have terrorized me without even touching me, just by playing mind games, hinting at what he might do, telling me what could happen to a little girl like me in New York City. He could have ditched me, which would have been truly terrifying in that era before cell phones. He didn't do any of those things. He was just an ordinary big brother with his little sister in tow. We met up with my parents at the appointed time in the lobby of our hotel, and that was that.

Except that later I got violently ill. My father stayed with me in the hotel room that evening when Mom and Mark went out to do whatever had been planned. Dad crouched behind me in the bathroom putting his hand on my forehead while I vomited into the toilet. I remember forcing my eyes to the left in between barfs so I wouldn't have to see the grossness in the toilet bowl, trying to make myself focus on the sink, its marble pattern and the little white bar of hotel soap in the corner with another bar next to it still in its gray wrapper. I remember how soothed I was by my father's touch.

The next morning I was better, and at breakfast we went through the usual suspects for my brief illness, the excitement of the trip, or something I ate, or maybe some nasty stomach bug and if it was that, we all hoped no one else would catch it from me.

At the end of that summer Mark left for college. He was out of my life, and I never looked back.

Seventeen

When Lathsamy moved out, she and Jeffrey agreed that Eddie would spend weekends with Lathsamy at her apartment. To start, Jeffrey would drop the boy off Saturday morning after breakfast and pick him up Sunday afternoon. If things went well they would gradually increase the time, through dinner on Sunday, eventually Eddie might come Friday evening and stay a full two days.

Some of this she talked about with venom, the sense of being on trial, having to prove she could handle the visits and earn the right to have more time with her son. But Jeffrey insisted. "He's acting in his professional capacity," she told me, her face clenched, her voice bitter as it always was now when she spoke of Jeffrey. "It's obvious. I'm like a protective service client to him. One more unfit mother for him to supervise. I have to show him I can be responsible."

Yet, despite all the feelings this brought up for her about Jeffrey, his judgments of her and his power in the situation, Lathsamy also saw it as a chance for a fresh start with Eddie. The separation was better for him, she said, better for their relationship. What could be worse than having a mother he saw every day but who had no real purpose in his life? Living together, the three of them as a family, there was nothing she could say or do with her son that wouldn't be overpowered by his relationship with his father, by Jeffrey's constant vigilance. Now she and Eddie would be having this time, just the two of them, making it possible for her to start being a mother again.

When Lathsamy saw me after Eddie's first weekend with her, she described it with a kind of determined enthusiasm. Eddie had explored his mother's new apartment, small as it was but still it had two closets, a space to crawl behind the couch, the bathroom with a tub with claw feet, the lower cabinets in the kitchenette, the nooks and crannies that hold special appeal to a four year old. They walked through the neighborhood, found a park with swings and a slide, went into Vietnamese shops, bought food for the two days. Lathsamy gave Eddie small tasks to help prepare meals. He had come with picture books that they read together. They went online to find computer games at Eddie's level. The couch folded out and they made it up together into a bed for the boy. To Eddie the weekend was an adventure. Lathsamy said that for her it was vindication, the best time she'd had with her son in longer than she could remember, proof if anyone needed it that she was capable of being a parent.

But the next week she called Jeffrey on Saturday evening and insisted he come for Eddie right then and take him home. She told me that after dinner she was doing dishes, the day up to then had been fine, very much like the first weekend, and now Eddie was sitting on the floor with Lathsamy's laptop absorbed in a computer game while she stood at the sink.

"I picked up a glass," she said. "The sponge was in this hand." She raised her right hand to shoulder level, extended it out in front of her, palm up, gave a small jerky shake to her head, slowly brought her hand down. "I was only going to wash the glass, Becky. Such a simple thing. Then I wanted to drop it. It was a thought in my head, but in my hand, too. My arm. I could feel myself lifting the glass up over my head. I could feel the glass leave my hand. The last touch of it as it slid from my fingers. I wanted it to break, Becky. I wanted it to smash in the sink." Frightened, she carefully put the glass down but found herself wanting to throw it hard against the wall; again she could feel the impulse as physical sensations, could feel the motion of her arm before anything had happened. She dismissed the impulse, forced her hand to leave the glass intact in the sink, turned around, took two short steps to physically move herself away. She stood there and breathed and tried to slow her heart, to contain her panic at these terrible things her body of its own volition had wanted to do, things she had actually done a year before, when she was Lulu, when she was out of her mind. She told herself she was Lathsamy. She told herself she was sane. She told herself she had resisted the impulses. She told herself she would be okay.

Lathsamy recounted to me how she had looked down at her son on the floor. "A sweet innocent little boy. That's what I thought, Becky. Like a little adult on the computer. He stared at the screen. He clicked the mouse. He made a small noise. It was a happy noise. He's my son and I love him. The next thing in my head was I could throw him out the window. I don't want to have these thoughts, Becky! How could I want to think something like that?"

The thought rippled through her shoulders and down her arms. It was so real, this physical capability in her to destroy her son. She lived on the third floor, she could do this thing and then stand there and watch him fall to his death. Her heart was racing, her body in turmoil. She couldn't look at her son, couldn't turn away from him, couldn't trust herself to make any move. There was some kind of poison inside her and she was terrified of her own self. All the windows were open, only the fine mesh of screens between what her body was capable of doing and the gathering darkness outside, the muggy August air through which her child would fall. Finally she lurched around the small apartment, slamming every window shut. Eddie allowed himself a puzzled glance at her before burrowing back into his game. Then she called Jeffrey.

In our session Lathsamy sobbed and sobbed, was beyond consoling, and the fact that she had stayed in control, had not acted on any of her terrible urges, had done the responsible thing by calling Jeffrey, had kept her son safe—none of this was a counterweight to what she had felt within herself, her own unbearable capacity for violence.

"Jeffrey was right," she said. "All along. He knew. He needed to protect Eddie from me. He knew what I am. I'm a monster. Only a monster could want to throw her little boy out the window." She wrapped herself in her own arms, rocking from side to side, her face streaming with tears. She said she should never have had a child. "I'm just a little girl. How am I supposed to be a mother when I'm only a little girl?"

There were no more visits for Eddie at Lathsamy's apartment. It was Lathsamy's decision. I don't think she ever got over what had happened. She was scathing in her judgments of her own inadequacy, her belief that she was a dangerous person, and all her rage at Jeffrey for having stood between her and her son she turned on herself.

They agreed that Lathsamy would have short weekly visits with Eddie at what was now Jeffrey's apartment. They agreed Jeffrey would be there the whole time. They tried having meals together, the three of them, but Lathsamy told me that they would sit awkwardly at the table, efforts at conversation sputtering and trailing away, until Jeffrey would slip into his old pattern of focusing on Eddie, playing word games or talking with him about some recent event, leaving Lathsamy feeling shut out exactly as she had when they were living together. It was hard enough, she said, to go back to the old apartment, but this was humiliating, unbearable.

They switched to having Lathsamy come for an hour or two to play with Eddie or read or do some kind of activity. Jeffrey was to be in a different room. It was a scaled down version of "just the two of them" for mother and son, and Lathsamy herself believed that this was as much as her own limitations would allow.

But even this became untenable. Lathsamy said she felt at a loss during these visits. Eddie's attention would wander, so unlike the curious, eager little boy who had come to her apartment in Dorchester, and she didn't know how to get him back. She felt Jeffrey's presence looming from wherever he was in the apartment, out of sight but very much in the minds of both mother and son, and it only made this worse when Eddie would scoot out to find his father and Lathsamy could hear their voices from the bedroom or study or kitchen that used to be hers. Everything was too familiar, the space was haunted and her failures closed in on her, and then she would hear Jeffrey tell Eddie to go back to his mother and it was just another kind of humiliation.

Finally there was an afternoon when Lathsamy and Eddie were sitting on the floor in the living room, reading a picture book about a mouse who was a dentist and had to climb up on a ladder to reach the big mouth of a fox with a toothache. Afterward Lathsamy remembered feeling that for once Eddie seemed actually to be there with her. "He was laughing at the story," she told me. "We were having a good time together. Then he looked up at me. There was a grin on his face. He said, 'Lathsamy, don't you think that's silly, a dentist on a ladder?' The breath went out of me, Becky. He always called me Mama. With all we've been through. Now suddenly I'm Lathsamy. He might as well have kicked me in the stomach."

For her in that moment the one word, Lathsamy, captured everything that had gone wrong, the vastness of it; here was her son telling her what she already knew but had wanted desperately for him not to know, that she was not a mother at all. "We were looking at each other," she said. "He was still smiling. He was waiting for me to answer. All I had to do was say yes, very silly, a dentist on a ladder. I couldn't say it. I started to cry. Once I started I couldn't stop. I knew it was a terrible thing I was doing. There are so many terrible things I've done to Eddie. Now this. How could I be doing this to him?" She tried everything in her power to gather herself. Then she would open her eyes and see the baffled little boy staring at her, and she would be overpowered by the sight of him, his innocence and the monstrousness of having brought him into the world. She couldn't say how long this went on before Jeffrey came in and gently picked up the boy and took him away.

After that Lathsamy did not go back. The best thing she could do for her son, she said, the only thing left to her, was to shield him from her presence, as if she were something toxic.

For two months Lathsamy and Jeffrey struggled over the terms of their separation agreement, caught in the kinds of arguments that many divorcing couples have when money is all that is left to struggle about, arguments that Lathsamy narrated to me week after week.

Without having any knowledge of divorce law, Lathsamy was counting on alimony, a thousand dollars a month, which she expected to go on indefinitely. She hadn't discussed this with Jeffrey before she moved. Lathsamy felt that Jeffrey had made a marriage commitment to support her; in so many ways he had not lived up to it, and the one remaining thing he could do was to at least make her life tenable financially. She was disabled, prevented by illness from working, even Social Security had recognized that. She was living in a tiny apartment in one of the poorest neighborhoods in Boston. She was relying on one last show of compassion, not even compassion, just decency and good faith from the man who had once devoted his life to her. Jeffrey countered that his income was modest, he now had one hundred percent responsibility for raising their son, and the child was his priority; besides, Lathsamy was an attorney and surely could still manage to earn some sort of income. To her, Jeffrey was poking at open wounds, yet again putting Eddie first, lacking the slightest understanding of how incapacitated she was.

I knew that I was only hearing Jeffrey's side through Lathsamy and he might present a different picture if he could speak for himself— but it wasn't my job to be objective. I thought of Lathsamy when she graduated from law school, not only how desperately her life had unraveled since then but also of how she had chosen one of the lowest paying types of legal practice, and how different her situation would be if she had made a corporate salary even for a few years. Now here she was, reduced to begging her estranged husband for enough support to eke out some kind of financial stability or else putting herself at the mercy of a legal system not likely to side with a mother who had left her child with his father—even less likely to take into account the crushing truths of Lathsamy's life. It made me furious and I had to rein in my feelings, make myself present to Lathsamy's own fury and helplessness rather than projecting mine onto her.

Things got even uglier when Lathsamy went online to look up legal information to do with divorce in Massachusetts. She found that the alimony guidelines would have Jeffrey pay seven hundred fifty dollars per month, but because of the length of their marriage, the law only required him to pay alimony for two and a half years. And under the guidelines Lathsamy, as the noncustodial parent, would have to pay Jeffrey almost two hundred a month in child support based on a complicated formula that left Lathsamy reeling. "Thirty months, Becky," she said. "That's how long I get alimony. But I have to pay child support until Eddie is eighteen. How can that be? How can anyone think that makes sense? It's absurd for me to pay child support at all. How can I support my child when I can't support myself? How am I supposed to live after the alimony ends? What kind of monsters make these laws?"

In the end, facing the prospect of having to hire attorneys, go through a contested divorce, and incur large legal costs that neither of them wanted to pay, Lathsamy and Jeffrey agreed to one hundred a month in child support and six hundred fifty in alimony. The alimony was to end in two and a half years, the one point on which Jeffrey refused to budge. In November they filed their separation agreement with the court, and after that Lathsamy spent our entire session going through all the ways she had been disregarded, degraded, victimized, screwed.

Eighteen

As the fall went on I had more and more the sense of Lathsamy's life closing in on itself. No marriage, no work, no visits with her child. Once the separation agreement was filed, no more reason to be in contact with Jeffrey. What was left?

She chanted twice a day. She went to meetings of her Buddhist study group but not too often, she had to travel so much further to get to the meetings and didn't like coming home alone to Dorchester long after dark. Her friend Ruth came to chant with her and visit almost every week, a few other women from the group less often. I suggested finding a group closer to her, but she didn't. Her weekly sessions with me she never missed. She went out to do food shopping once or twice a week. Otherwise she stayed home in her small space. She watched TV. She slept.

She was cutting more, as much as three or four times a day she told me, sometimes on the underside of her arms, sometimes close to her wrists. But never deep enough to be dangerous, she said. Still, every week I asked if she was suicidal. She always said no.

In January Lathsamy and Jeffrey appeared in court and the judge approved their divorce. A week later she complained to me that her next-door neighbor was coming into her apartment whenever she went out. She said she could detect the woman's odor, discovered small things missing, a magazine, a coffee mug. The door to the bathroom would be closed when she was sure she had left it open. She would find her bed made when she remembered leaving it unmade. I asked if she was locking her door when she went out. Always, she said. And was it still locked when she got home? She said that it was, which proved that the neighbor had managed to get a copy of her key.

Lathsamy's next complaint was that cigarette smoke from the unit below her was coming up into her apartment through the floor boards and radiator. I had no reason to doubt this was true, but she also believed that the person downstairs had started smoking to poison her. She fixated on it. "No one should have to live in these conditions," she said. "It's not a home. It's a prison. People say I could go out....But how am I supposed to go out? for hours at a time? in the middle of the winter?...If I go to the library people look at me. I know what they're thinking. She doesn't belong. She's crazy...." Besides, she added, the more time she spent out of her apartment, the more opportunities it gave to the woman next door to invade her space and mess with her things. Lathsamy's face, already sagging, crumpled into the bewildered face of a lost little girl. "Why am I being punished? I don't bother anyone....Why are they doing this to me?"

She was trapped in a situation that was rapidly becoming impossible. She couldn't stand the smoke, she was sure she was being psychologically assaulted by her neighbors, she had nowhere to go, everything was out of her control.

It was similar to her paranoia during the spring and summer of her surgery, but also different. She continued to call herself Lathsamy, not Lulu. She did not dress provocatively, did not go out to bars or otherwise seek men. She showed few outward signs of agitation. She sat still through our sessions, spoke slowly, softly, sadly. If there were aspects of mania in her wild accusations, in her fixation on the malice of her neighbors, she was manic in slow motion, and large swaths of depression remained. Instead of rampaging, she was flailing, imploding. She talked about having reached the end of the line, but denied any plans to kill herself. I tried very gently to raise with her the idea of going into the hospital. She wasn't willing to consider it. She wasn't committable, not dangerous to herself or others, just living in Hell.

In February there was an evening when Lathsamy's neighbor, ironically the same one she believed had been entering her apartment, became concerned because she heard Lathsamy's shower running for what seemed like too long. As I would later learn from hospital records, when the neighbor knocked on Lathsamy's door there was no answer, but she could clearly hear the water. A half hour later she knocked again, called out to her. Still no response. The woman phoned the landlady, who agreed to come to the building. The landlady used her key to open Lathsamy's door, and she and the neighbor found Lathsamy unconscious, naked on the floor just outside the bathroom. When the EMTs came, her body temperature was 88 degrees. A few more hours and she would have been dead.

We were never sure exactly what had happened. Lathsamy would later tell me that the last thing she remembered was getting undressed to take a shower. The hospital reported that her blood sugar and thyroid were wildly out of control when she arrived at the ER. Her weight had dropped below one hundred pounds. It was likely she had become too disorganized to take her insulin and oral medications correctly, if she was taking them at all, and who could say when she had last eaten.

This time there was no premature release from the hospital. She was in intensive care, then put on a medical floor, then sent to the psychiatric unit, still paranoid, psychotic, grossly unstable. Altogether she was in the hospital for three weeks. Her medications were adjusted, then adjusted again. When she got home she had stopped being delusional but was far from well. Physically, verbally, emotionally, if anything she was even slower than before her hospitalization. She said she was exhausted all the time, making challenges of the most basic tasks. Her hands shook. She was understandably afraid to get in the shower. She was easily distracted. She seemed to be in steady decline.

Later in March, there was a morning when Lathsamy's friend Ruth went to her apartment to chant with her. She rang the buzzer and nothing happened. She called Lathsamy's phone, went into voicemail. Then she randomly pushed other buzzers until she got someone to let her into the building. Lathsamy's door was ajar, Ruth went in and found her slumped on the couch, barely conscious, an empty bottle of Klonopin by her side. Not enough to kill her. Later Lathsamy said that she had decided to take all the pills in one of her several bottles of medication and see what would happen.

She was hospitalized again, another ten days, came out looking not much different. And that was to be the pattern. Through the spring and into the summer Lathsamy was in and out of the hospital, though she made no more suicide attempts or gestures. Instead there were times when she asked to be hospitalized, others when she accepted suggestions from me, or from her psychiatrist, that she was not well enough to be at home. I think none of us had realized how much Jeffrey's presence, for all her railing against him, had helped to hold her together, Jeffrey and also Eddie when the three of them had been living together. By herself, she appeared to be crumbling. The change in her attitude about going into the hospital seemed a matter of resignation, a weariness with life and struggle, and in that sense maybe not so far from suicide.

It was hard to see how these revolving door admissions would end, how she could pull out of the downward spiral, but by the end of the summer she did. I never really understood it. Did the doctors finally come up with the right mix of medications? Maybe so. But many meds had already been tried and they were running an uphill battle against the diminishing of Lathsamy's spirit. Now it was as if she called a truce with herself. Or maybe it was something else entirely. Regardless, somehow she managed to stabilize, and after the summer she was never hospitalized again.

Nineteen

When my parents arrived I brought them down the long hallway into the kitchen. I've been in my apartment for seven years and I can count on one hand with fingers to spare the number of times Mom has been here. The last time was three years ago. I invited them for Sunday dinner, I thought if I tried to act more like an adult, I don't even know, I must have hoped something good would come of it. From the minute my mother walked in the door she started criticizing, when was the last time I painted, the floors needed sanding, how could I live with such old furniture, she went on and on, nothing was right. By the time we sat down to dinner I was livid and then she wanted to know where the meat was. I had made a chickpea dish with rice and a salad and she went off, how could I be serving such a meal, what did I expect her to eat.

Now against my better judgment I was hoping again for something good to happen, only this time the stakes were so much higher. In the kitchen I parked my parents at the table, my mother at the end nearest the doorway, my father with a window behind him. I offered Dad coffee which he accepted with a worried smile. My mother was going to be more difficult, naturally, she doesn't drink coffee and I offered her tea knowing she wouldn't like any of the herbal teas I had, and she asked for black tea knowing I wouldn't have it. She settled for a glass of water.

I had to force myself through these civilities, make myself take deep breaths. I sat down at the table across from my father, Mom to my left, and I realized that we had managed to replicate our seating arrangement from all the years at home. For all the ways that my kitchen is nothing like Mom's—it's half the size and there is no open space to speak of, the fridge is in the corner to the right of the table and the stove and sink against the wall opposite the window, I use pegboard which my mother would never touch in a million years—despite every last detail of this space being different, we were expressing through the physical location of our bodies that it didn't matter where we were, we bore the same relation to each other.

"All right, Rebecca," my mother said, her voice already jagged, "why don't you tell us what this is all about."

Of course she doesn't bother to ask about last night, what was wrong with me, am I feeling better, and I really want to give her shit about it, but I need to let that go. I've been trying to figure out how to say this for the last hour and I still don't know, so I just fucking say it. "Mark sexually abused me when I was little."

Mom's face, already clenched so tight I thought it couldn't get any tenser, manages to tighten even more; she stares at me ferociously and she says, "What are you talking about?"

I glanced at my father. He winced, shifted his weight, looked down at the table. "There was a gap between when I would get home from school and you would get home from work, do you remember that, Mom?"

She shook her head, a series of quick jerking motions.

"Well there was, and that's when it happened."

"It, what are you talking about?"

"I'm talking about rape, Mom. Mark raped me. I was eight years old and he raped me."

"Why are you telling me this now? Don't you know this is the day before Thanksgiving? Don't you know how much I have to do today? They're all back there sitting in my house. We're supposed to go to the Science Museum in two hours!"

"Leah..."

"You stay out of this!" she snaps at Dad, the same words, the same piercing voice I've been hearing forever.

"Mom I'm telling you now because I only just remembered what happened."

"What are you talking about Rebecca? Remembered when what happened?"

This is becoming surreal, but here we are and I don't know what to do except to keep telling her this thing she can't hear. "After I got to the house last night, Mark said something that triggered my memories of him raping me."

"Triggered? What do you mean, triggered?"

"Something happens in the present that makes you aware of an event from the past. A traumatic event."

"A traumatic event, and this happened, what? Thirty years ago did you say?"

"Yes Mom, when I was eight."

"And you wait all this time to tell me? After thirty years you have to bring this up the day before Thanksgiving?"

"I didn't wait thirty years, Mom. I forgot. I only remembered this last night."

"What are you telling me, something bad, something upsetting happens to you as a child and you forget about it for thirty years? How can that be?"

"These things do happen, Leah," my father manages to say in a quiet, careful voice.

"Don't you tell me about things happening. The great expert, the famous psychologist, now you're going to sit here and tell me what happens and what doesn't happen." My mother looks like someone who is being assaulted. "Doesn't anyone here understand what day it is? Doesn't anyone have any consideration for what I have to do in the next twenty-four hours? Don't you see I can't deal with this now?"

What I want to say is, Mom how about once in your fucking life having some consideration for me, how about just this once letting something be about me and not you. I can hear the words in my mind, I can feel them slipping down the chute from my head into my throat where I swallow them.

"I didn't choose when to remember," I say quietly.

"But you chose to call your father and have him drag me over here! Why couldn't you have waited until after Mark and Christine and the girls leave? Two days! What would two days have cost you? Why couldn't you have just shown me the consideration to wait until I can get through Thanksgiving?"

There are so many feelings running through my body I can't keep track of them, and behind all of them I know that this is completely futile, the thing I am trying to do, to ask this woman who I can see with my own eyes and feel with my heart is incapable of hearing what I am telling her, who speaks the truth when she says she can't deal with me, with my insane demands on her, and the thing I am trying to do is only to ask her to be my mother. I am going to fucking ask her anyway.

"Mom. I want you to tell Mark to leave your house."

"What?" She stares at me, she hasn't stopped staring at me for the last ten minutes, but now it feels like a drill boring through my eyes and into my skull.

"I want you to send Mark away."

"What are you talking about? When? They're only here until Friday, Rebecca. They're leaving in two days."

"I want you to tell him to leave now."

"How can you ask me to do something like that? They came here for Thanksgiving! This is the one chance I have in the whole year to see my grandchildren."

"He raped me when I was a little girl, Mom. I was eight years old and he was twice my size and he raped me over and over. I want you to tell him there is no place in your house for a man who raped your daughter. I want you to stand up for me."

Now I am crying, I don't want to be but I am; I don't want to be showing this but I am, and for the first time my mother has lowered her gaze and I look again at my father and I want something from him. In this moment when I know what my mother cannot possibly do, I want something from my father and I don't know what—and then I do know, I want him to say he believes me, just that, and he will not meet my eyes and he says nothing.

Then my mother looks up, also in tears and she says, "Rebecca, why are you doing this to me?"

November 26

BECKY CLIENT: Mark, Mom. Fucking Mark and Fucking Mom. Both of them, I was talking to fucking stone walls and Dad sits there useless and this is my fucking family, that is all there is to it, and let's take a fucking inventory: we have the older brother who rapes me when I'm a little girl and now denies it to my face and has the fucking what? has the fucking is there even a word? to say I'm being obscene, my obscene lies and how he'll fucking destroy me and I cannot even fathom how that word can form on his disgusting foul asshole lips, obscene obscene obscene shit shit fucking shit! who is obscene, Mark? who is the fucking obscene one around here? I just want to scream I want to smash things I want to crush him in my fucking hands!! I do, you think I'm just saying it, I want to put my fingers around his throat and squeeze all the air out of that obscene body; I am what he fucking made me and I do, I have this inside me I could use my own fucking hands and kill him, and listen to me, *listen to what is coming out of my own fucking mouth, look at what I am reduced to, look at what he has done to me one more time, he always finds a way to fucking win and him on top and me below, and I just want him off me, I just want him fucking off me. Get off me Mark get the fuck off me get your fucking foul filthy hands off me, get your big ugly disgusting body off me, get your fucking penis out of me, get off me get off me get off me get off me get the fuck off me....*

BECKY THERAPIST: *Becky, for so many years you didn't remember what Mark did to you. All that time for you it never happened, and now you're being raped all over again, Mark is on top of you and his penis is inside you and no matter how hard you try you can't get him off. Your whole life has been swallowed up in this horror. You have so many terrible feelings that make you want to scream and smash things and kill him, it must be...*

BC: *I'm not gonna kill him, you know that, right? I'm not gonna try to choke him, right? I'm not ever gonna be in the same room with that fucking man again. The same state. The same fucking universe.*

BT: *You feel like choking him and killing him but you won't ever do that, you just want to stay as far away from him as you possibly can. Yes, I know that.*

BC: *Yeah, and where does that leave me, I have all this burning energy, this fucking rage and what the fuck am I supposed to do with it and I never even finished the fucking inventory of my lovely family...*

BT: Can we stay with Mark for a little while?

BC: What?

BT: What it's like for you, having him on top of you, being under him. Can we stay with that?

BC: Are you out of your fucking mind?

BT: I'm wondering if we can find a way for me to be there with you?

BC: Be there with me? What are you talking about?

BT: You're so alone down there. You've been so alone with this for the last thirty years.

BC: Yes, fucking right I'm alone with this. So, what, you want to shovel your way down into this shitpit and get raped with me? Share the fucking pain?

BT: I'd like to hold you.

BC: Why would you want to do that?

BT: It's my job.

BC: Quite a job you have there.

BT: It's the best job in the world.

BC: What if I don't deserve to be held?

BT: I'd like to hold you anyway.

I can't fucking stand it! And I lied, okay? about the key, I didn't swallow it and here I am opening my big stupid mouth one more time because who could watch all this shit and just be a Silent Miss Two Shoes? Not me, I can tell you that, I'm gonna give her a piece of my mind for all the good it's going to do, which is nothing.

All she can talk about or think about or write in her stupid journal is Mark this and Mark that and how she wants to strangle him, well hello, I've been wanting to get my hands around his neck for thirty fucking years and where did that ever get me? Nowhere, that's where, just locked up in this stinking dungeon and guess who threw away the key for real. And yeah fucking Mark is still on top of her, well I could have told her that if she would just for one tiny millisecond listen to me, but she never ever listens to me, and yeah her mom is a fucking bitch and yeah her dad is a pathetic asshole and I could have told her that too but no, she has to do things her way and stumble through life in the dark and this is what she gets, big surprise.

So now one lightbulb after a fucking nother goes off and she still doesn't know I'm here. How is that even possible? I know she's clueless but this is like a whole nother dimension in time and space. What am I supposed to do? Smack her in the face? Right, I wish. Scream my lungs out? Like anyone would hear me from down here in the dungeon. Even if I was up there, I could be two inches from her ugly nose and she still wouldn't see me.

Why should I even be surprised? Well I'm not surprised, okay? Why should I even care if she acts like I don't exist? Well I don't fucking care. I just hate it. I hate every single thing about her. I hate every single thing about me. I hate every single thing about all of them. I hate every single thing about being alive.

Twenty

I would exaggerate if I said that Lathsamy rallied during that fall. Truer to say, she kept her head above water. She told me she was taking her life a day at a time, the commonplace phrase from addiction recovery which she applied to her own struggles, and for a time it served her well. She focused on mundane things within her grasp and reported small successes, staying out of the hospital for another week, keeping her weight above a hundred pounds, managing her medications, maintaining stable blood sugar, cleaning her apartment. She had a polite conversation with the woman next door, thanked her for having helped her. She said with pride that she had gone to the library, went about her business there without worrying what people thought of her, took out a book by Barbara Kingsolver and was able to read thirty pages in one day.

She surprised me, and I think herself, by visiting Eddie for Christmas. She went not on the day itself but the weekend before. It had been 15 months since she had seen her son and she was anxious whether he would remember her, but of course he did. She bought him a big battery powered fire engine with flashing lights and a siren, and she worried about that too, having told me she had no idea what to get a five year old boy for Christmas. She carefully wrapped the box in glittery white paper with reindeer and when Eddie tore off the paper, his eyes got big and he happily played with the truck for ten, fifteen minutes, running it across the floor and making up a story about a six-alarm fire and heroic firefighters who saved everyone in the burning house. Then she worried that the noisy alarm would get on Jeffrey's nerves, but he smiled and seemed pleased to see the boy enjoying his present.

Once again Eddie called Lathsamy by her name. But this time she expected it and wasn't thrown out of balance. No tears, no drama, only a pleasant visit. She stayed for an hour. Once Eddie was done playing with the fire engine she asked him about Kindergarten, which he had started in September, and he cheerfully told her about his best friend and second best friend and third best friend and his favorite things at school, story time and art and recess. If he was baffled to see her after all this time he didn't show it. Jeffrey spoke to her without hostility, made small talk, eventually said he was glad to see her. Before she left the three of them sat at the table and had dietetic cake which she understood Jeffrey had bought in consideration of her diabetes.

Afterward when Lathsamy recounted the details of the visit she was calm, thoughtful, seemed relieved that it had gone well, but there was also something deeper, a sense of peacefulness. I thought it might open a door to bringing her son back into her life.

In the new year Lathsamy turned reflective, more so than in years. She talked about her village in Laos, her mother and father, herself as a little girl. Who she might have been if she had lived her life there. Her memories were still only fragments and her image of herself as a woman in Laos had the same quality, a series of still frames. An illiterate peasant woman living in a hut with a dirt floor. Married to a farmer. A brood of children. Brothers, sisters, nieces, nephews, cousins. Her own parents, her husband's parents, the grandparents of her children. No computers, no cell phones, no television, a simple traditional life. A village where people don't think of themselves as poor. The cycles of weather, monsoons and dry seasons. An intimacy with nature. The constancy of the river, its steady flowing, the catching of fish.

She talked this way for weeks. She was grieving. I believed it was a healthy grief, something she needed to pass through to set the stage for a new direction in her life. I was reminded of a poem I love called "The Definitive Journey," I mentioned it to Lathsamy and told her the first line, *I will leave. But the birds will stay, singing.* She nodded, got a little teary, and asked for a copy of the poem which later I gave her.

A few weeks after that Lathsamy brought me a poem. It was the first time in years she showed me something she had written. The first thing I noticed was how shaky her handwriting was, large painstakingly formed letters, uneven on the page, like the writing of a child and in such contrast to her neat graceful script when I first knew her. Then I started reading and was swept up into her words.

In the Present: 9/11

Above us, clear sky, corn silk blue
A perfect day for flying.

We are surrounded by
glass and flames, flashing,
as we hover on the edge.

Pushed by heat and panic,
we grab hands to jump.

No net

Others go before us and with us.
Many will remember.

It is a long way down,
Yet our time is short.
Hard surfaces wait to greet us.

As I step off, I notice the touch of your hand.

"Lathsamy, this is beautiful," was the first thing I said.

She nodded, her face soft and sad, and didn't say anything.

"Do you want to talk about what it means to you?"

"It doesn't mean anything to me, Becky."

I thought, This has to mean something to you, or many things. You showed it to me, that's not for nothing. Just the one line, no net, doesn't that speak volumes about your life? The hard surfaces, the time being short, the entire September 11 metaphor, if that's what it was, a metaphor. The touch of someone's hand—whose? I took a breath and what I said was, "Had you been thinking much about 9/11 before you wrote this?"

"I didn't write it," she said. "It was a gift from the universe. Please Becky. Accept it as a gift."

Part of me wanted so much to argue with her. I understood what she was saying, that the source of the poem was something larger than her. At the same time the words related so poignantly to Lathsamy's deepest struggles.

But the part of me that prevailed said that respecting Lathsamy to decide what she did or did not want to talk about, did or did not want to acknowledge, respecting her in every possible way was the backbone of our relationship and she needed the safety and security of our relationship far more than any understanding or exploration of her struggles I might manage to push her into. More than anything I wanted to be her net.

"All right," I said. "I accept it as a gift. Thank you."

In March Lathsamy shifted again. She started to talk about money, worried about what would happen when her alimony ended. That was more than a year away but once she began to go there she couldn't let it go. She told me there was no way she could manage without alimony. Even with it her savings were dipping; she couldn't understand why because she only spent on essentials and yes she could try to be more careful and keep up her bank balance. "But when Jeffrey stops sending me a check every month," she said, "then what? After my rent, do you know what's left from my Disability check? Two hundred dollars. Who could live on that? My savings will go, it won't matter how much I have in the bank. Then what will I do?"

I gently asked if she thought she might be able to hold a part time job.

She shook her head. "I have to be realistic, Becky. I have to look at myself as I am."

We talked about government programs, food stamps and fuel assistance, she supposed she could apply for them but it still wouldn't be enough. She would be reduced to going to food pantries. How could she live like that?

Lathsamy's desperation about money rekindled bitterness toward Jeffrey, her sense of betrayal. How could he possibly have put her in this position? The man she once loved. The man who when he heard about the horrors of her childhood had opened his heart to her, or seemed to open his heart. "Really what was I to him?" she said to me with a quick flash of her old anger. "An exotic Asian woman? The heroine of a story about evil and suffering? The former sex slave. I allowed him to believe he is a good man. I allowed him to step around his own pain." Lathsamy's view of Jeffrey was that he had created a version of her in his own mind, a romanticized ideal that served his own needs and couldn't possibly stand up to the reality of the person she was. She said that even if he hadn't exactly used her, he was willing to let her sink. "Another year and I won't be his problem anymore. That's what I've become to him. A burden. The man I had a child with."

It was one more instance, to her, of the general trend of her life. The little girl torn from her home to be used for the sick pleasures of men. The invisible teenager. The false success. The inability of anyone to grasp, to tolerate the truths of her life. Her own shameful behavior, her abandonment of her child. The sheer volume of destruction that humans were capable of. "People are so ugly," she said to me. Then she caught herself and added, "Not you, Becky. But everyone else."

I told her I thought there is ugliness and beauty in all people. That is something I truly believe but it came out sounding like fluff and she shrugged it off.

Looking back, it was such a clear signal and I know all about hindsight, but still. It was only a month since she had given me the poem about jumping out of a burning building. I did ask if she was suicidal, but not because I was picking up on anything in particular, only because the question had become a routine part of our conversation, too routine, and she gave me her usual answer, no. I'm not sure what else I could have done, but there must have been something.

The second Friday of April, Lathsamy didn't show up for our session. In ten years she had never missed an appointment. I phoned her, got voicemail, left a message asking her to call back. Twenty minutes later I tried again, went into voicemail again, left another message.

I didn't have her landlady's number so I called the police and asked for a wellness check. Two officers went to her building. Her door was unlocked. They found her on her bed, unresponsive, her arms and sheet covered with blood, much of it already congealed, deep slashes in both wrists. No pulse. The bottoms of her feet were turning black. At the emergency room she was pronounced dead. She did not leave a note.

Twenty-one

Thanksgiving morning. The phone rings, I pick up and my mother's voice is shrieking into my ear. "I hope you're satisfied, Rebecca. You've ruined my Thanksgiving."

"Mom? What are you talking about."

"They're gone."

"What? Who's gone?"

"Mark. Christine. April. Martha. They left this morning."

"Where did they go?"

"How should I know? Home. Mark changed their reservations. They got on a plane this morning and went back home."

My mind is racing to keep up with the words. I want more than anything to believe that my mother sent him away, that she did this for me, and I know it can't possibly be true. "You didn't tell Mark what I said. Did you?"

"What are you talking about?"

"You didn't tell Mark to leave." Not a question anymore, a statement of fact.

"Why would I do such a thing? And ruin my own Thanksgiving?"

"Then why did they leave?"

"How should I know? Mark said something came up, some unexpected business. As if he would have business on Thanksgiving."

"Then..."

"It's because of you! Isn't it? Didn't you talk to him yesterday?"

"Yes..."

"You see!"

I don't know what to say. I don't know what to think, what to feel. Mark actually left because I told him to? After how he talked to me on the phone? I don't believe it. Nothing is making sense. But he really did leave, that's what Mom is telling me and she may be many things, but she is not going to make something like this up.

Meanwhile my mother seems satisfied that she has made her point. "So Rebecca," she says in a different, practical voice, "I'm planning to serve the meal at three. What time will you be here?"

She can't be saying this. After yesterday, after having not an ounce of sympathy or empathy for her own daughter's sexual abuse, after just now telling me that I've ruined her precious Thanksgiving by having the gall to stand up for myself and speak the truth, after all that she expects me to come and sit at her table? It's laughable. It's deeply serious. I feel my body clench into something fierce. This is one thing I can control. "I'm not coming Mom."

"What are you talking about, you're not coming?"

"I'm not."

"But Mark left! Isn't that what you wanted?"

"Yes. It's what I wanted."

"Then why aren't you coming?"

"After the way you treated me?"

"How did I treat you, Rebecca? Tell me what I did?"

There is no way I can tell my mother what she can't hear. I just went through this with her yesterday. Not again. I say, as calmly as I can, that it's something I'm not able to explain. Predictably she asks me how I can accuse her of mistreating me and then refuse to say what she did. I tell her she's right, I shouldn't have accused her of anything, I apologize. So you'll come, she says. No, I say. I'm not coming.

I can feel my mother flailing, the weight of her desperation. "You're really not coming?"

"No Mom."

"How can you do this to me? Do you have any idea how much food I have in this house? What am I going to do with all this food?"

My whole life I had spent every Thanksgiving with my family—but not this one. The thought freed something in me, I took a breath and felt it go deep into my lungs, felt the rise and then the fall of my stomach. It was my body in that moment, no one else's. It was, suddenly, my day.

Not that I believed for one second that anything was resolved. Just that there was a crack, a small space I might squeeze through and have a day of my own.

I threw on my jacket and was out the door. I walked up the bike path to Alewife. The late morning was gray and chilly, the trees mostly bare, no snow on the ground yet. I pulled on my knit hat, drew my scarf a little tighter. I didn't pass anyone on the path. This was my familiar route to work, now it was all mine. I found it comforting, the sense of belonging to this unremarkable little stretch of pavement and grass and trees.

From the MBTA station I walked along Alewife Brook Parkway, normally a busy road but today the traffic was sparse, people undoubtedly heading to their Thanksgiving destinations, as I was in a different way heading to mine. I passed the Fresh Pond Mall on my left, then a smaller shopping center on my right, the parking lots almost empty, the feel of a ghost town. At the first rotary I veered to the right onto Concord Ave, crossed it, and found the short path through a small wooded area that would take me to Fresh Pond.

It's a small reservoir, protected from intrusion by a chain link fence around the perimeter. I gazed through the fence at the dark choppy water, felt wind glide off the open expanse of the pond and brush my face. I was glad to be there, in contact with these simple forces, water and wind. I turned to my right and followed the trail that skirts the pond. After a few minutes I saw a woman up ahead with her dog; as we approached I could see it was a golden retriever off the leash, running ahead and waiting, running ahead and waiting. The woman was older than me, her head uncovered, short graying hair and a weathered face, and she nodded as we passed; I nodded back and then they were behind me.

As I walked around the pond I found myself thinking about my pregnancy for what seemed like the first time in days, or was it weeks? It had been such a driving force, the impossible choice, the torment of it and then it was swallowed up by that quick succession of events, the nightmares and then the reality underneath them, these truths I had been hiding from for so long, and I realized something obvious that I had managed to miss: my pregnancy had led me to face the truth, to begin to understand who I am and what my life has been. It was my first glimpse that there might be something other than awful about being pregnant. It didn't bring me any closer to knowing what I would do, but somehow it helped me, also for the first time, to feel easier about it. I knew there was a way this didn't make any sense. I only had a month left to decide, and when I looked at the particulars of the decision nothing had changed, I still didn't feel I could take the life of my unborn child and I still didn't feel I could be a mother—if anything less so than ever with what I now knew about my history, the horror I carried in my body and my spirit. It wasn't rational, it was something felt, this easing and loosening of a knot that had been binding me to a spot where nothing seemed possible.

From the far side of the pond I walked down Fresh Pond Parkway to the Charles, and then along the river, and there my thoughts drifted and settled on Lathsamy, not because of anything to do with the river but to do with the space this day was opening for me. It was the first Thanksgiving since her death and I let myself ache with the loss of her. Ten years, this woman I loved, and there was only loss now, and the only thing left was to grieve. I felt her with me, in all of her phases, the burning eyes and the sad sagging face; I thought of her history and of my own and I knew that my grief for Lathsamy was blurring into something I felt for my own lost self, Lathsamy as a little girl in a village in Laos, Becky as a little girl in a house in Newton, the promise of both of these lives before each of us was swept up into things for which words fail, swept up and crushed, and I let these losses blur together and let myself ache.

I walked and walked, following the river through a last bit of Cambridge and on into Watertown. I saw hardly any people. From time to time small clusters of mallards paddled past me heading downstream. Occasionally the thrum of sparse traffic would stop entirely and there would be silence, not a true silence but this rare absence of city noise and I could hear the sweep of wind through branches and their remaining brown leaves, the soft lapping of the river against its bank. It was as close to a sense of peace as I think I could come, living in this body, this spirit that had not known peace in thirty years.

When I got home it was dark. Later that evening I called Hannah, hoping she would be done with her Thanksgiving event, and I was a little surprised when she picked up, and pleased. I asked how her day was. She laughed and said she survived. Hannah is from California, her husband is local with a large extended family and I've been hearing for years how out of place she feels with her in-laws. This day was no exception.

She asked about me, assuming I'd have my own tale of family holiday stress, same as every year. Instead I told her I didn't go, and she asked why, and I said a blowout with my mother, and she said I was always having blowouts with my mother so this one must have been a real doozy, and I said yeah, a doozy. Then I told her how I did spend the day, and Hannah said, "Honey, you should have told me, you could have come with us." I knew her sentiment was not entirely altruistic, that my presence would have made things easier for her, and I was touched anyway.

Part III

Moments of Truth

Someday I'll be dead. Except I don't really believe it. It's the only way I could ever escape from this fucking dungeon and get out of the hellhole of my own self. Not to mention getting away from her, the FB. It's my only hope and it seems too good to be true. Knowing me I'll probably live forfuckingever.

Twenty-two

Lathsamy's body was cremated. There was a memorial service for her in early May, organized by her friend Ruth. During the weeks after her death I plodded through our relationship, heavy with the sense of having failed her. If it had been a colleague whose client committed suicide I'd have been the first to tell her not to carry the burden of responsibility for another person's choice, that you can't keep someone alive who is determined to die. I tried to say this to myself but it felt hollow and wrong. It hadn't been a question of keeping Lathsamy alive against her will. My purpose was to help her find within herself the will to live. That was the point.

There were so many critical moments, events that one after another unraveled her life but could have happened differently. I should have anticipated when she decided to tell her story to the sex trafficking conference, what it could unleash. I should have helped her prepare for it. Before she had surgery for the tumor on her kidney I could have talked to the surgeon, explained how fragile Lathsamy was, worked with him to put together a post-operative plan to integrate physical and psychiatric recovery. Most of all I should have realized that Lulu was burrowed inside her the entire time before she burst out into the open. I should have invited Lulu into our sessions, given her a safe place to rage, held her the way a mother holds a tantruming little girl.

I always wanted to see the best in Lathsamy. After her death I had to ask myself how much I was holding out a truth to her about herself and how much it was my own need to make her into a person she couldn't live up to, a kind of self-deception. That had been one of her complaints about Jeffrey, that early in their relationship he had idealized her. Why couldn't I see the ways I had done the same thing? My need to believe that horror can be surmounted or transcended, my own unwillingness up to the very end to see how much damage had been done. Whatever I let myself take in, the truth was worse.

The memorial was held at the Soka Gakkai community center in Boston. A bright, warm spring day, the weather of renewal, the ground and trees bursting with life. Inside we gathered in a large, plain room with bowls of fruit placed in front of the large scroll of the Gohonzon at the altar. I arrived early and sat near the back, watching people filter in, some greeting each other with hugs, their faces somber, voices hushed. There was no one I recognized until Jeffrey came in. He was alone. He spoke briefly to a woman in a long dark skirt, accepted a handshake from a man who approached him, nodded to something that was said, then sat half the room away from me. I thought of going over to him but didn't.

The service began with the same Buddhist ritual I had witnessed at Lathsamy's wedding, a woman standing in front and leading the group in chanting nam-myoho-renge-kyo and a more elaborate chant called Gongyo. I thought of Lathsamy sitting in front of her altar every morning and evening for so many years, chanting these words, how she talked about her Buddhist practice as the thing that kept her alive, and then I thought of her slashing her Gohonzon during the terrible summer after her surgery, how the Gohonzon in that moment had become a representation of her own body, a kind of presentiment, and I began to cry. I was aware that many of the people near me were in tears. A woman two seats to my left, a stranger, reached across the empty space between us and briefly put her hand on my arm.

When the chanting ended a tall, thin white-haired woman stood at the podium set off to one side of the altar. She said her name was

Ruth Weber. So this was Ruth. She started with things you would expect her to say, that it had been her honor to be Lathsamy's friend, how intelligent she was, how courageous. The tragedy of a life cut short. But then in a steady voice she talked about things not often mentioned at a funeral. The events of Lathsamy's childhood. Her mental illness. Emotional pain beyond Ruth's comprehension. The simple awful truth that Lathsamy had taken her own life. Even from where I sat in back I could read the sorrow on Ruth's face, the depth of it.

Ruth invited others to speak who were moved to do so, and a steady stream of people came up to the podium. One after another they spoke about how Lathsamy had touched their lives. I had assumed that almost everyone there was from the Buddhist community but I was wrong. There was a woman who had known Lathsamy in law school. Colleagues from the Boston court where she had practiced. A judge. A teacher from Eddie's preschool. The neighbor who had helped to save Lathsamy's life. And Buddhists as well, women and men from her study group.

After the service food was laid out on tables at the rear of the room and people milled and talked quietly, and that was when I spotted Lathsamy's adoptive parents from New Jersey. I hadn't noticed them arrive. They stood at the far left of the rows of chairs, the bald man in a gray suit and blue necktie, the woman in a plain black dress, her aging face and neatly arranged blond hair fresher in my memory than I would have expected. As I approached I thought I saw the same baffled expressions I remembered from the time, so many years ago, they came to my office with Lathsamy. I was wrong about that too. They greeted me warmly, knowing who I was but having forgotten my name. I had forgotten theirs also and we introduced ourselves again. Ken and Hilary. To my surprise they told me that Lathsamy had stayed in contact with them, never more than once or twice a year, but still they were aware that she had married and had a child, and later had sensed she was not doing well though she had not let them know about her hospitalizations or divorce. Ruth, who had taken on the responsibility of going through Lathsamy's belongings, had found their email address and something else that managed to convey their role in her life.

"She's a very kind woman, Ruth," Ken said to me. "It was a beautiful service."

"We are just so grateful we could be here," Hilary said. "There was so much we didn't understand about her. This gave us a chance to know her a little better."

When we were done talking I looked around for Jeffrey, didn't see him and had a surge of anxiety that he had already left. Now it felt important to connect with him and I regretted not having done it before the start of the service. Then I saw someone at the far end of the room near the door, a man with his back to me. I walked in that direction keeping enough to the side to be able to see his profile and it was Jeffrey after all. He was standing with a woman in a dark pantsuit who I recognized as one of the people who had spoken at the service, an attorney I thought. She was doing most of the talking, gesturing with her hands, slightly hunched at the shoulders, and Jeffrey listened to her and nodded. I waited at a distance, trying and failing to locate exactly what I wanted to say, and when the woman turned away I walked up to him.

I doubted he would recognize me. We had met in person only once and then very briefly, in the lobby after the sex trafficking conference, at a moment when Lathsamy's mental state was abruptly shattering. But Jeffrey greeted me by name. We had talked on the phone so many times that I felt I knew him, though of course all I really knew was how overwhelmed he had been by his wife's relentless crises. We had formed an alliance of sorts in the service of things neither of us had been able to accomplish, a manageable life for Lathsamy, a tenable marriage. Now here he was, a middle aged man with a neatly trimmed beard, black streaked with white, wire rimmed glasses, deep circles under his eyes, creases running the width of his forehead, a sad stricken face.

Jeffrey said how much he appreciated having been able to call me when things were desperate, how I always returned his calls and was such a steady presence, how important I had been to Lathsamy. In turn I appreciated how much he had cared for her, the endless challenges, how impossibly painful it must have been for him. These were polite things we were saying to each other, not dishonest and not formalities but with the flavor of condolences, and it seemed to me that maybe this was enough, that words were not really the point, what I had needed, and possibly what Jeffrey needed also, was simply to stand for a short time together in this physical presence. Something simple and human, being here in the same place and time, the two of us who from such different places had loved Lathsamy so much.

Then Jeffrey said, "You may have wondered why I didn't speak during the service."

"I didn't wonder," I said. "As an ex-husband..."

"It isn't even that. Not exactly. This is hard to say, but the truth is—I'm angry at her. It's not all that I'm feeling, but....People were up there being so honest. How could I stand in front of a hundred people and say that I'm angry at someone whose life was hell?"

Wrong again, what I took for sadness on his face was a more complicated grief, sadness and anger and other feelings I could only guess at. "Angry because of Eddie?"

"Yes."

"Of course you're angry."

"How could she do this to him?"

It wasn't a question I could possibly answer. Eddie had seen Lathsamy only once in the year and a half before her death, which may in some way have cushioned the blow but it would be foolish to believe it could be anything but devastating for a child his age to lose his mother, let alone lose her to suicide. It was something Eddie would be dealing with for the rest of his life, an event he would need to successively take in and grieve and move on, only to reach a new stage where his mother's suicide would have an entirely new meaning and depth, where he would wrestle yet again with the exact question Jeffrey was asking, how could she have done this? How could she have done this to me? How could I have meant so little to her?

All I could think was to ask how Eddie was coping.

"On the surface he seems fine," Jeffrey said. "But there's no way he can really be fine. I worry about him all the time."

"Yes, of course you do."

"We had our own service after Lathsamy died, my parents and Eddie and I. We lit candles and looked at pictures. We told stories. Eddie held the toy she gave him for Christmas, I imagine you knew about that? I can't say what it means to him, his mother's death. I talk to him about her, I ask about his feelings, and I still don't know. I'm having him see a therapist."

It was as if the word cut my flesh, a therapist. A lot of good it did his mother, I thought, seeing a therapist. I knew I was being too hard on myself and yet this was the end result, Lathsamy dead at thirty-eight, my own age, and here we were at her funeral. This was not Jeffrey's concern, my raging guilt. Of course Eddie should be seeing a therapist, a good one I hoped.

I tried to shift my focus to Jeffrey's situation, not my own, and I said, sincerely, "Eddie is lucky to have you for a father."

Jeffrey blinked and looked away, and I pictured his son, an innocent little boy who could be loved but could not be shielded from the crushing weight of his mother's history, and when Jeffrey turned back to me tears were streaming down his face and now I was the stranger reaching across an open space to rest a hand lightly on his arm, and as I did something heaved in me and let go again and we stood there and cried together.

Twenty-three

The day after Thanksgiving I went back to work. Some of my Friday clients were away for the holiday but I had rescheduled others from earlier in the week, so my day was full and it was a relief to be focusing on other people's problems. After work I walked home along the bike path, less peopled than on a normal Friday but not deserted like the day before, and still I carried in my body the feeling of yesterday's walk, the solitariness and the sense of belonging.

That evening I nestled onto my couch, wrapped in a shawl, and watched a DVD. A Chinese film about an aging woman who had been the servant of the same family for most of her life; she was housekeeper but also had been nanny to children who now were grown, and only one of them, a middle-aged man, was left. The tenderness, the bond between the old woman and the man grew on me as the film went on, and finally I got it that she was more a mother to him than his own mother. I was moved and teary when the phone rang. I thought about letting it go into voicemail but I hit pause on the remote, checked the caller ID on my phone and picked up.

"Hi Dad." I heard it come out dry, noncommittal and yes, there was an edge of anger.

But whatever my voice might have been expressing was completely lost on him. "Becky. Look. Listen Becky, I thought you should know this. I told Mark to get his ass out of my house. My own son, goddammit. I wanted you to know. I mean Jesus H. Christ.

I told him, he's not welcome in my house. You have a right to know this, Becky. Becky, look. I need to talk to you. Can we talk, the two of us? Not with your mother, you know what she's like. Listen, can we talk?"

I could picture my father squirreled away in his study, a drink in his free hand, slouched in his chair, eyes slightly narrowed, grinning at what he took to be the eloquence of his own words. "Sure Dad," I said, "but not on the phone."

"No, Jesus, not on the phone. I'll come to your place. Can I come to your place?"

"Yes, but not tonight." The thought of him driving in this condition.

"When? Tomorrow?"

We agreed on the next morning, ten o'clock. After we hung up I wondered if he would remember.

I didn't know what to make of his call, except for my revulsion at how drunk he was, a reaction that you could say was strange or more than that, unfair, given how much drinking I've done. Maybe it was revulsion for myself as well, maybe to do with my memories of being a little girl and the fucking Happy Cokes. But my father telling Mark to leave, what did I feel about that? I had to believe he really did this, it was the only way my brother's departure made any sense; and no matter how many sheets to the wind Dad was I didn't think this was something he would say if it wasn't true. So it meant he had actually come through for me, didn't it? It was an amazing thing my father had done. Wasn't it? I should be feeling good about this, great about it, supported beyond what I had thought possible. Instead I felt anxious, bewildered. Why did he wait two days to tell me? Why did he need to get drunk to make the call? What would he have to say when he was sober?

Saturday morning. My father rings my buzzer at ten on the dot. We sit in my living room, me on the couch, him on my old wooden rocking chair. We had a chair something like this one when I was growing up, it was my father's favorite, he would call it his rocker and sometimes when he sat in it he held me on his lap. He would eat potato chips scattered on a paper plate, drink a beer in a tall glass and watch the news, and I would snuggle up against his body and rest my cheek on his shirt and smell the beer from his breath. Now he starts to rock just perceptibly, probably not even aware of the motion. Behind him morning sunlight streams into my apartment.

"Becky. Well, first of all. I want to apologize for last night. I shouldn't call you in that condition."

"No you shouldn't."

His eyes shoot a quick flash of surprise; I don't think he has ever heard me answer him so sharply. Then it's gone. "No. I feel bad about it."

I nod. I wait. He collects himself.

"Look. I know that what you were telling your mother about Mark... well, what you were telling both of us. I know what you were saying is true."

"How do you know, Dad? Do you mean that you believe me?"

"Well. Of course I believe you. But no, I mean more than that."

"What?"

He breathes. His eyes dart one way and then another and finally settle on the couch just to my right. "There was an afternoon. It was during this period of time that you were talking about, when you were eight I suppose, eight or nine. My last two appointments of the day, you see, both of them canceled. I had nothing left to do at the office. So I came home....Look, don't you remember this?"

"Remember what, Dad?"

He winces, lets out a breath. "Right....I came in the front door, I called out hello the way I always do. You know. No one answered. I wondered where you were. Mark, well, he was a big boy, he would be out with his friends after school. That's what I thought, you see. But you should be home, that time of day."

"I could have been at a friend's house. Sometimes I did that."

"Well, I didn't know. I thought it strange when you didn't answer. I looked in the kitchen. No sign of you. Then I went upstairs. I could hear something going on in your room. The door was closed. I knocked, you didn't answer. I knocked again. I called your name. I could hear...well, there were noises of some sort. It didn't sound like you. It sounded like someone older, someone—not noises a girl would make. I opened the door. I found Mark on top of you, down on the floor....You don't remember?"

"Mark being on top of me?"

"No, not that, of course I know...I mean—you don't remember me coming into the room?"

I close my eyes, try to picture it, find nothing. Which makes no sense. Why would I have remembered what Mark did to me, so many little details, the physical sensations of his abuse, and have no memory of my father coming into my room that day?

"No Dad, I don't remember. What did you do?"

"I pulled Mark off of you."

I try again to remember, what it must have felt like for that heavy weight to be lifted from me. The sudden relief of it. Nothing. "Then what?"

"I took him to his room."

"And?"

"Well. I wanted to beat the shit out of him. That's the truth, Becky. You know I never raised a hand to either of you."

"So did you? Beat the shit out of him?"

"No. I didn't. It took every ounce of self..."

"Then what did you do?"

My father stops rocking, leans forward. He tents his hands, pushes both index fingers into his lips, lets them drop. "I told him never to touch you again. I told him if he ever did I would send him away."

"Send him away where?"

"Oh—to a boarding school, I imagine."

"You imagine? Is that what you told him?"

"I think so. Yes."

"A boarding school. Not a juvenile correction facility? It had to happen again to send him away? You didn't tell him you were going to call the police? You didn't call the police?"

He pulls back, his head first, then the rest of his body, the physical impact of this onslaught of questions. "The police?"

"Yeah, as in, to report a rape?"

"There was no rape that day, Becky. Now I know, there were other times. But you have to understand, I didn't know that then. How was I to know? That day I stopped him before—well, before anything could happen."

"Anything, Dad? Mark lying on top of me, a fifteen year old boy crushing an eight year old girl's body down on the floor, that isn't anything?"

"All right, yes of course. But you know what I mean."

"I don't think *you* know what you mean, Dad. I understand what you think you mean, but you don't know what the...you really don't know what you're talking about."

For the first time he bristles. "That's not fair, Becky."

"Not fair? You tell me what's fair, Dad."

He looks at me, opens his mouth, shuts it. He's getting pissed and he doesn't want that, he didn't come here to argue with me as if I were Mom, I'm his daughter and something terrible has happened to me and he wrestled with many demons to get himself into this room. He really believed he was coming here for me, doing this to relieve some part of my awful burden, and instead I'm giving him shit and he doesn't know what to do with me. I feel all these things broadcasting out of him and I am not going to take care of him. I am going to keep giving him shit.

"Dad," I say, "was Mark, was he undressed?"

Now he's the one trying to picture it. "I don't remember."

"You picked him up off me and you don't know if he was wearing clothes?"

"No." He lets out a sigh. "I don't."

"Well let me help you. By the time Mark was on top of me he was never wearing clothes."

"All right."

"Yes all right. So there you are, you've just hoisted this big fifteen year old boy off a little girl, the boy is stark naked, you take him to his room, and you tell yourself you got there in time to stop anything from happening?"

"Yes."

"And what exactly made you believe he hadn't already raped me?"

"Well. When you put it that way..." He fidgets, looks far to his left toward the windows, the row of houseplants in front of them, gleaming in the morning sun. "I take your point, Becky. But at the time..."

"At the time what, Dad?"

"At the time I believed I had stopped him."

"And did you ask him if this had happened before?"

"No. I didn't."

"You just assumed it hadn't."

His face is crumbling. He doesn't know what to say. I feel like I'm beating him up. I don't know what else to do. I have so many more questions, what did he do to make sure this would never happen again, did he tell my mother, was he aware of the gap between when I got home from school and when Mom got home from work, did he have any idea the risk I was at. But I already know the answers. He didn't do anything else to make sure it wouldn't happen again, he assumed that giving Mark that talking-to was all that was needed, no he never told Mom, yes he was vaguely aware of the gap, no he didn't think it was a problem, no he didn't think I was at risk, and so the questions are really accusations, straps of leather to slap him in the face, and I have already done so much whipping and I know it serves no purpose. I just want to stop. I feel the tears welling in my eyes.

I realize there is only one question left that matters. I know the answer to this one too, but I need to hear him say it. "Dad. After you were done with Mark. Did you come back?"

"Come back?" The look on his face, he is completely lost.

"Yes. Come back to my room. Come back to me, to be with me."

"I see." He meets my eyes for the briefest instant, gives a little nod, then stares at something above my head, or at nothing.

"Well?"

His face sags, his shoulders. He has only the wrong answer. There is nothing else he can say. "No. Becky. I didn't."

"Why not Dad?"

"I thought I had done what you needed me to do."

"Which was?"

"Well. To take Mark off you."

"To stop the rape."

"I don't know that I even thought of it in those terms. That word."

"To stop anything from happening."

"Yes."

"And it didn't occur to you that there was a little girl lying on the floor of her room, that her big brother had just been on top of her, completely naked, that whether or not quote unquote anything had happened the little girl might be frightened, the little girl might be terrified, the little girl might need comforting, the little girl might need support, the little girl might need words of kindness, the little girl was your own daughter and none of this occurred to you?"

I'm sobbing now and my father is a blur but I can feel him crawling in his own skin, feel how far I have taken him beyond any kind of pain he can tolerate. "Becky...I don't know what to say."

"Let me guess. When you left Mark's room you went downstairs and poured yourself a drink."

"It's possible."

"Yes. It's possible." I'm whipping him again, I know it and this needs to stop. I need this to stop. Just one more thing. "Did you ever talk to me about it after that? Dad?"

He waits. He gropes the air. "No."

"Why didn't you?"

"I thought....You seemed fine, Becky. Why bring up something that, you know. Well. That would only disturb you."

"Better to leave sleeping dogs lie."

"I suppose." The weariness in his voice. Under that, so much fear. "Something like that."

Now I am truly done. There will be more time to cry afterward, more time than I can measure. I wipe my face with my fingers, then with the heels of my hands. I surprise myself at how quickly I calm down, bring myself back into the room, bring my father back into focus. An aging man, elegantly dressed, his mustache neatly trimmed, sitting there helplessly on an old wooden rocking chair.

"I'd like you to leave now, Dad."

"Becky..."

"Please."

He nods, not knowing what else to do. He pushes himself off the chair. Now he meets my eyes, desperate for me to do something that will make this all right. There is nothing that can make this all right. He brings his teeth down onto his lower lip. I imagine he is searching for words. He can't find any. He lifts his hands, palms up, and lets them fall. Finally he turns, walks slowly out of the room. I hear his footsteps creak through the hall, and then the door opens and closes.

Sunday morning Hannah texted to ask if I was okay. She said she'd been worrying about me since we talked on Thanksgiving, she couldn't imagine what must have happened between my mother and me. I texted back that I wasn't okay and it wasn't just about my mother. She asked if she could come over. I said yes.

We talked for hours. I told her everything I had remembered, what had happened with Mark at my parents' house, on the phone, my conversations with my mother, my father. I cried and cried. She held me. She apologized for having been so self-absorbed recently. I

told her that if we were having a self-absorbed contest I would win.
Then I told her I was pregnant.

Twenty-four

For ten days after Thanksgiving weekend, my life returned to a semblance of normal. Days were taken up with my work. Hannah called every evening to check on me; she said she was going to keep doing it until I told her to butt out of my life but I gladly accepted her support. I had no contact with either of my parents which was a relief beyond words. We all seemed to take for granted that I would not be coming to Sunday dinner and if that broke the pattern of my old normal, it was one welcome change.

But against this backdrop of external calm, on the inside I was churning. How could I not be? The truth of who I really am, that phrase kept coming back to me during moments when there was nothing else needing my attention. If I had been living all my life until now with a fiction about my father, the last thirty years had been filled with an even larger lie about me, the construction of a false self. I understood this was something I did as a child in order to survive, and then it took on a life of its own, never a conscious choice. It didn't matter. False is false.

Who was this woman I had made up? A woman who'd had a mostly ordinary childhood. A woman whose biggest problem in life was that her mother was too needy and narcissistic to accept her for who she really was. A self-aware woman who knew what her own needs were, knew what it was inside her that craved acceptance. A woman whose father made up for most of what she didn't get from her mother. A woman who had not experienced serious traumas. A woman who took charge of her sex life. A strong professional woman. A woman who could take alcohol or leave it. A woman who was leading a good, solid, meaningful, rewarding life.

Now, in place of this appealing self-portrait, I knew my life was shit. A plain unappealing truth, but it was also a square of solid ground. I didn't have to pretend anymore, didn't have to try to make it any better than it was. What was the point? I am a woman whose life has been shit for the last thirty years. That was shorthand for many things, years and years of suffering I had been trying so hard to shield myself from, and the shit, the suffering was my self. It felt important to say this simply, baldly.

The suffering that was my self. The self that was my suffering. Who was she? I had been circling around her these past weeks, coming closer and closer, in my dreams, my vomit, my rage. In my journal. I could feel her inside me, a physical presence. Another kind of presence too, one I didn't have a word for, the messy stuff that sticks together to make a self.

Inside me was a little girl. She has been in there all along. The little girl who has carried the terrible weight of this suffering all by herself for so long. If my father abandoned her, then so did I. I had been running from her with all my might for thirty years. It was time for me to do what my father had not, to find my way back to that little girl.

December 2

BECKY THERAPIST: Hello 8 year old Becky. Welcome.

8 YEAR OLD BECKY: Welcome? Are you serious? Where have you been for like the last thirty fucking years?

BT: It sounds like you're really angry...

8YOB: Don't give me any of that therapy shit! I'm hearing you say bladdy-blah and all that high and mighty therapist talk, as if it makes you the queen of the fucking world. Maybe you can pull the wool over their eyes, your clients or whoever the fuck, but you don't fool me, lady.

BT: You don't want me to tell you what I'm hearing you say....

8YOB: I don't want you to play therapist with me! I see right through you! You're Fucking Adult Becky!

ADULT BECKY: All right, so you want...

8YOB: I want you to answer the fucking question!

AB: You want me to say where I've been for the last thirty years.

8YOB: Yes! Agghh!

AB: I've been neglecting you, 8 Year Old Becky. I've been trying to push you away.

8YOB: Well at least she admits it.

AB: I don't want to push you away anymore.

8YOB: Like it matters what you say.

December 3

ADULT BECKY: Hello 8 Year Old Becky.

8 YEAR OLD BECKY: You again?

AB: Yes.

8YOB: Why don't you just leave me alone?

AB: Like I did for the last thirty years?

8YOB: Yes! Like you did for the last thirty fucking years.

AB: Why...

8YOB: I know what you're going to say, I'm a mind reader in case you don't know, and the reason is because you're just going to shove me back down into the dungeon as soon as you get tired of me.

AB: You don't trust me.

8YOB: Give me one good reason why I should fucking trust you?

AB: I can't.

8YOB: Hah! You see! She admits another one!

AB: But what if I don't get tired of you?

8YOB: What if! What if the moon was made of cheese, would you eat it? What if a fucking nuclear bomb hit Boston, then we'd have nothing to worry about. What if IT never happened?

AB: You mean if Mark hadn't...

8YOB: Yes I mean if Mark hadn't!

December 4

8 YEAR OLD BECKY: Okay, if you're going to insist on these whatever they are thingies happening every day, I'm going to give you a piece of my mind. You are a Fucking Bitch. There, I said it to your face and why shouldn't I because that's exactly what you are. Now have you had enough of me? Now are you going to send me back down to the fucking dungeon?

ADULT BECKY: No, I'm not going to send you back to the dungeon.

8YOB: But you've had enough of me. Right?

AB: I haven't had enough of you.

8YOB: You lie like a rug.

AB: You don't believe me.

8YOB: Well yeah, that's what I just said, isn't it?

AB: Yes.

8YOB: You're scared of me, aren't you?

AB: I have been scared of you.

8YOB: What's that supposed to mean, you're not anymore?

AB: I'm working on it.

8YOB: You're what?

AB: I'm less scared of you than I was.

8YOB: Still a little scared, right?

AB: Yes. A little.

8YOB: That's because I'm such a badass.

AB: It's more that I'm such a wimp.

8YOB: Well that's the fucking truth. First sensible thing I've heard you say.

AB: I do think you're a badass.

8YOB: Second sensible thing I've heard you say.

AB: I think you have every reason in the world to be a badass.

8YOB: Don't go making excuses for me lady. I'm a badass because I suck.

AB: I don't think you suck.

8YOB: Go fly a fucking kite.

December 5

8 YEAR OLD BECKY: Had enough of me yet?

ADULT BECKY: No.

8YOB: Well maybe I've had enough of you.

AB: You're still really angry at me.

8YOB: Well yeah.

AB: It's fine that you're angry at me. It's great that you're expressing your feelings.

8YOB: Don't you start telling me what's fine. And don't you dare tell me what's great about me or any fucking thing. As if there was anything great about me or what I do or what I say or what I fucking feel. Who do you think are, lady? Just keep your fucking hands off of me and my feelings and my fucking life.

December 6

8 YEAR OLD BECKY: Okay, I'm going to ask you something. Where the fuck were you when I needed you?

ADULT BECKY: You mean...

8YOB: Yes I mean!

AB: I don't know where I was.

8YOB: What the fuck? How can you not know?

AB: It's complicated.

8YOB: Then forget it.

AB: It seems like the important thing is that I wasn't there when you needed me. I didn't help you say no to Mark. And I didn't help you afterward.

8YOB: Just like you know who.

AB: Yes. Just like Dad. I left you all alone, we both did.

8YOB: All alone. All fucking alone. Do you have any idea what that means? Do you have any idea what it's like to be locked in a dungeon for thirty fucking years?

AB: I can imagine, but I can't know it the way you do.

8YOB: That's right you can't.

AB: Would you tell me?

8YOB: Tell you what?

AB: What it was like for you to be locked in the dungeon all that time.

8YOB: You really want to know?

AB: Yes.

8YOB: No you don't.

AB: It's okay if you don't want to say.

8YOB: Don't you fucking tell me what's okay and what's not okay. I'll decide what to tell you and what not to tell you. Maybe I want to tell you about the fucking dungeon.

AB: Right, you've had no say at all for the last thirty years and I'm the one who kept you locked in the dungeon. Now it's up to you...

8YOB: Yes it's fucking up to me, that's what I just fucking said!...You want to know the worst of it? You don't but I'll tell you anyway. I deserve to be in the dungeon. Want to know why? Of course not but I'll tell you that too. It's because I'm a piece of shit.

AB: You feel like a piece of shit...

8YOB: It's not just a feeling! Don't fucking do that! I AM a piece of shit!

AB: Okay.

8YOB: Why would you even want to be here talking to me?

AB: Because you're inside me. You are a part of me. I tried so hard for so long to get away from you and look where it *got me.*

    8YOB: *Where did it get you?*

    AB: *Right back to you.*

    8YOB: *So we're stuck together.*

    AB: *Yes. We're stuck together.*

December 7

    8 YEAR OLD BECKY: *Sick of me yet?*

    ADULT BECKY: *No. I'm not sick of you. I'm glad to be here with you.*

    8YOB: *Glad?*

    AB: *Yes.*

    8YOB: *You should have your fucking head examined.*

December 8

    8 YEAR OLD BECKY: *Still here?*

    ADULT BECKY: *Yes. I'm still here.*

    8YOB: *Had your head examined yet?*

    AB: *Not yet.*

December 9

    8 YEAR OLD BECKY: *Still here?*

    ADULT BECKY: *I'm still here. And I'm so glad to be with you.*

Twenty-five

Thursday, the end of the afternoon. I have just left my office when my cell rings. Mom. We haven't spoken in two weeks, since I told her on Thanksgiving Day I wouldn't come for dinner. It's the longest I've ever gone not speaking to my mother. Now my body clenches top to bottom at the sight of her on my caller ID. I don't pick up.

I wait until I get home to listen to her message. All she says is I should call her right away. I try to read her tone. Her voice is wired. Which could mean anything, there's not a day in her life when she isn't tense.

I know I have to call her and I find myself wishing I could have a drink first. That's an urge I haven't had for I don't even know how long, to have a drink, and I realize it would be the worst thing I could do, even if it was an option, to numb myself out before I talk to her. I want to be clearheaded. I want to feel all this shit.

What actually is the shit I'm feeling in this moment, phone in hand, about to speed dial my mother? I'm feeling compelled. I have to call her, those were the words I said to myself only a minute ago. The truth is I don't have to. It's a choice. I take a breath, then another. I do what I can to center myself in my body, to unclench. Then I make the fucking call.

She says she wants to see me. I ask if we can't just talk on the phone. No, she says, in person. Why, I ask. It's too important for the phone. What's so important? She'll tell me when she sees me.

She wants me to come to her house which is fine, I really don't want her here again but we haggle over when. She says can I come now. Silence for two weeks and suddenly she has to see me instantly, and for dinner no less. There's no way I'm going for dinner, this is already weird enough without sitting at the table with her and Dad. Finally we agree on tea at 7:30.

When I arrive Mom opens the door. I'd been bracing myself for my father, he's always the one who answers the bell. Mom's mobility has decreased steadily with age, and besides I think they both have come to an understanding over the years that starting out with Dad helps to ease me into the house, a grudging concession to reality on my mother's part. Except that tonight it's not at all clear Dad would be easing me into anything. I haven't spoken to him either since that morning he came over to talk, Thanksgiving weekend. Did he actually tell Mom about our conversation? It's hard to imagine. But everything to do with my family has become hard to imagine. All I know is what I see before me, Mom not Dad.

She thanks me for coming. I ask how she is.

"The same," she says, dismissing the question with a wave of her hand. "Why would I be any different." Then she channels her energy into labored steps and we walk slowly, quietly to the kitchen.

Still no sign of my father. Finally I ask and Mom says he's out for the evening. So that explains that. Undoubtedly off with some woman younger than me, doing what he does.

She tells me to sit and offers me a cup of Lipton decaf. I had been taking tea as a figure of speech. I have never known my mother to keep anything but caffeinated black tea in her house, which she knows I won't drink. I was fully expecting her to offer it to me anyway. I would refuse, she would persist, eventually I would wear her down and she would resign herself yet again to my being unreasonable and ungrateful. Instead she has broken the pattern. The truth is that Lipton decaf is hardly any better, it still has caffeine, just less, and I wouldn't drink it anywhere else. But I fight off my reflex to say no.

She's made this effort. The least I can do is accept it.

Mom hobbles around the kitchen, wending her way through the pouring of two cups of tea. The mugs are already out on the counter, the kettle on the stove, and still it takes her what feels like forever. Each task is a major effort, opening a box to take out a packet, extracting the tea bag from its packaging, crossing the floor to the stove, lifting and tipping the kettle. She brings my cup to the table, fingers wrapped around the handle, her other hand resting on the lip of the mug to steady it, one cautious step at a time, manages to ease it down onto the table in front of me without spilling a drop, then lets out a long sigh, gathers herself, turns and navigates back to the counter to go through the same routine with her own tea. It's hard to watch but I don't turn away, I have spent too many years of my life looking through this window trying to will myself out from under my mother's presence. I know better than to offer to help. So I sit here, trying to let myself take in how far her physical condition has deteriorated, waiting for whatever the hell is coming.

Finally Mom drops into her seat. She's breathing hard. "Everything exhausts me," she says. "You'll have to give me a minute, Rebecca."

"Thanks for the tea, Mom."

She nods, doesn't try to say anything else while her breathing gradually slows. I sip my tea. I think about how much I can leave in the cup without seeming rude. Then I look at my mother for some hint of what this could possibly be about, anything in her face, the way she holds herself that might be at all different, the suggestion of a change in her attitude toward me, and I find none. The same inner sagging, the same resignation, the same bitter reproach in her eyes—directed not just at me for failing her as a daughter, but at the world for everything it has done to her. I'm here, she asked me and I chose to come, but what good can possibly come from this?

When she's ready my mother shifts her eyes toward me and says, "Sam told me what your brother did to you."

"Dad told you?"

"Yes, he..."

"Mom I'm the one who told you what Mark did to me."

"What do you mean?"

"I mean that you came to my apartment the day before Thanksgiving and I told you what Mark did to me."

"Rebecca, I don't understand what you're trying to tell me."

It has taken thirty seconds for my mother to make me feel crazy. She truly has no idea why I'm saying this. The concept that I might have a reaction to her believing Dad but not having believed me, this seems completely outside her frame of reference. She's looking at me, her eyes are desperate, she's stranded. I'm doing this to her and I'm doing it to myself and I am stranded, just like her. The last thing in the world I want to be and it's what I am—as bad as her, clueless. All I want is for her to see what it does to me that she'll believe my father, her lifelong nemesis, before she'll believe me. All she wants is for me to stop this relentless campaign to be who I am, to have these impossible feelings. Here we are, I'm desperate for her to be someone she's not, she's desperate for me to be someone I'm not. Two peas in a pod.

How can I explain a fraction of this to her? I can't. I take a breath, I let it out. If she were my client I would empathize with her. I can't do that either. She's my mother, not my client.

"Never mind, Mom," I say, and I feel the tension in my jaw ease the slightest bit, though I really don't know why it should. "You asked me to come because you had things to say to me. Dad told you what Mark did. Okay, what else?"

"Rebecca, I know what happened the day before Thanksgiving."

"I'm sure you do."

"Then your father went and talked to you."

"Yes."

"I didn't know. He doesn't tell me anything."

"So when did he tell you?"

"Yesterday."

"He waited almost two weeks?"

"Apparently."

"Why did he wait so long?"

"How should I know? What does it matter?"

I hear five decades of bitterness in her voice, a lifetime spent living with a man who has no regard for her. It's true, how would she know. "You're right, Mom." How long has it been since I have told my mother she's right? "It doesn't matter."

Her face somehow registers that I've agreed with her about something, anything. I feel more than see the subtle loosening of muscles that have been bound so tight. She looks down at her tea, lifts the mug to take a small sip, and there is a tremor in her hand as she sets it back down. She meets my eyes and says, "Rebecca, I can't stand it, what your brother did to you."

It should be the most natural thing in the world, a mother's outrage at her daughter's rape. It should be the most natural thing for a daughter to be comforted by her mother, for the daughter to dissolve into tears. This is so far outside what I expected that I can't even try to understand how Mom could have said what she just said. I barely notice the thoughts telling me not to trust her words. Trust hardly seems to be what matters. There is only what is happening right now, and putting names on all these feelings is so beside the point, they are all liquid and running together and pouring out my eyes.

Once I'm able to, we have an actual conversation. Mom asks me why I didn't tell her what Mark was doing to me at the time. I explain that I believed it was my fault; he had convinced me I would get in horrible trouble if I told. I give her more details, not about how he got me to whip him, I'm not sure I will ever be ready to tell her that, but I describe some of what he did to me psychologically, the alcohol he gave me. I describe how I learned to shut off my feelings. It must have been terrible for me, she says, to be so alone with this, just a little girl. I nod and let myself cry again. How could there ever be an end to these tears?

"Mom," I say. "How come you didn't see that something was wrong? All those afternoons when I was sick?"

"You were a child, Rebecca. Children get sick."

"And Dad never said anything to you? Back then?"

"Oh, your father." She waves her hand, clearing the air of him. "Don't start."

"At least you know now. Finally."

I realize that Mom's breathing has gotten fast and shallow again, the labor of this real conversation, the toll of this terrible knowledge. I ask if she's okay and she nods. She drinks her tea and we sit quietly, a different quiet than I can remember between us. I'm not fending her off. She's not clutching at me. Our eyes keep meeting and when we don't hold this gaze we keep coming back.

Out of the silence I say, "I want to tell you something Mom. It's going to sound harsh but it's real. Okay?"

"All right, Rebecca. If you feel you need to."

"I want to."

"All right." She says it with a lift and drop of her shoulders. In that same gesture a half hour ago I only would have seen fatigue and resignation but now I feel something else from her, some kind of willingness to hear me.

"For so long I have felt unloved by you. I've acted it out in a hundred ways but until now I couldn't just say it."

"Unloved?"

"Yes."

"When you were born you were my treasure, Rebecca. No mother ever loved her little girl like I loved you."

This must be true, not the literal comparison to other mothers but what Mom is really saying, the intensity of her love for me then. It's not even that hard to imagine. "I believe you."

"You don't know the half of it. After—you know it was seven

years between your brother and you. Two years after your brother was born, I miscarried. Then I got pregnant again. I had a stillbirth."

"Why didn't you ever tell me?"

"What was to tell?"

She's jarring me back into the old picture of her, the woman with no sense of a child's needs, the distorted ways that things untold get communicated. "This is part of my history, Mom! I had a right to know."

"Rebecca, what are you talking about? It all happened before you were born."

What use would it be to try to explain that her history is my history? She hasn't turned into a completely different person. I have to rein myself in. "Okay....Thank you for telling me now."

"I want you to understand what it meant to me, when you were born. To have a girl, after all those pregnancies."

"Your child who was stillborn, was it a girl?"

She nods. She looks so sad. Forty years and the loss is so present. "Did you name her?"

"A name? What sense would it make?"

"It could have helped you to grieve, Mom."

"What was to grieve? She was gone, that's all."

My mother doesn't know how to grieve, she only knows how to suffer. As soon as I think this I know how obviously true it is, how much weight she has carried, how many ungrieved losses. This starts in my head as a criticism but what I feel is something else, pain for her pain, my own grief for the kind of life she's led, so many things that have always been beyond her grasp. No one would choose to live this way.

"And then I was born and I made up for her?"

"You were the joy of my life, Rebecca. For eight years, I couldn't ask for a better daughter, until..."

"Until Mark raped me."

"How could he do such a thing? My own flesh and blood?"

"I was your flesh and blood too, Mom."

"All these years, I didn't know. When he did that to you, I lost both my children."

Lost both her children. For my mother this drama is about Mark as much as it is about me; it should have been obvious but I see this now for the first time. Since I walked into this house and sat on the couch with Mark's daughter and he stood there above me and I remembered everything, I have only wanted Mom to understand what was done to me, to hear me and soothe me and for once behave like a real parent, and now that against all odds she is actually doing this I realize how blind I have been to the other half of her story, what it must be like for a mother to find out that her son raped a little girl. It strikes me like a physical blow. No wonder she couldn't take it in when they came to my apartment the day before Thanksgiving. I thought it was because she didn't know how to be a mother, I thought it was because she cared more about her fucking Thanksgiving than she did about me, I thought it was because she had no emotional capacity to attend to anyone but herself. There may have been truth to all of those things but what I completely missed was that in order to hear me she would have to face the truth of who Mark is. Now she has done this, has somehow found within her heart the strength and the courage to let herself lose her son.

My mother had both her hands on the table, pressing down as if to prop herself up. I shifted my body so I faced her directly and moved my right hand, really without any hesitation, until it rested on top of hers. I could say I found myself doing this, that my hand moved of its own volition while I was a detached observer, but that isn't true. I chose to do it.

Her skin was surprisingly soft. She trembled to my touch, a subtle rippling of muscles, and then stilled.

"What it's like to be a mother, Rebecca, you can't know. The heartache."

"Maybe I will know."

"What are you talking about?"

"Mom." I smiled at her, for the first time that evening, the first time in decades. "I'm going to have a baby."

Twenty-six

I didn't know I'd made the decision until the words were out of my mouth, sitting with my mother at the kitchen table, but since then I've had a clarity I wouldn't have thought possible.

I still write in my journal, but I've also started going to an actual therapist, one with her own body and her own office who I see every week and pay each time with a check. Her name is Jane and she is a wonder. I must have interviewed fifteen therapists before I settled on her. I knew I would be a handful and that I needed someone who is equally adept with kids and adults, because I've got both in me. Eight year old Becky is still testing her like crazy, but the thing is that Jane isn't scared of her. She seems to know what life is like for a little girl who was raped and then abandoned for thirty years. She doesn't expect my little girl to like or trust her and she has endless patience, though she's not afraid to set limits where they're needed, like no saying fuck you. Mostly I feel safe with her. She takes me as I am. I don't know what else I could ask for.

I've joined a support group for expecting single moms. There are eight of us and we cover a wide spectrum. Some of the pregnancies were intentional, some not. I'm not the only woman in the group who struggled with whether to keep her child, and no two of us resolved this in the same way. I'm certainly not the only woman who's been sexually abused. So we share a lot and at the same time we have all kinds of differences: age and class and race and so many of the circumstances of our lives. But the main thing is we are all facing the same challenge and when any one of us talks about her fears and hopes, we are all right there with her because we carry those same fears and hopes in our bodies. We plan to keep the group going after our babies are born. It may not be a village, but it's as close as we're going to come to one.

I don't know if I'm having a girl or a boy. I've had ultrasounds but I choose not to look at the screen and I ask my medical people not to tell me. There will be time enough for gender after the child is born, but for now I just want this to be a life. I've also chosen not to have amnio. If I'm carrying a child with birth defects, so be it. I haven't come all this way to turn around and destroy a life because it doesn't conform to someone's idea of normal. Who the fuck is normal, really?

I think of Lathsamy, who had at least as much clarity as I do about having a baby. If you plotted a curve of Lathsamy's recovery and decline, the birth of her child would have to stand out as the decisive turning point. At least that's how it seems to me now as I anticipate the birth of my own child. She was so determined to turn poison into medicine, the Buddhist notion of transforming suffering into an affirmation of life. A way to redeem her childhood by using it to guide her toward the creation of a good life, a child who would be loved and honored and protected. Instead her history crushed every capacity she had to be a good mother, or to be a mother at all. Abandoned as a child, she abandoned her own son, first in life and then in her death. She didn't mean to harm him, she did it because she reached points where there was nothing else she could do, she had exhausted all other options and was reduced to reenacting what happened to her as a child. It's chilling, especially because Lathsamy was someone I so deeply loved, and maybe too because, despite our being the same age, there were many times and ways I felt like a mother to her, and if this was the best I could do with mothering someone I loved, what does it say about my capacity to mother my own child?

I want in every inch of my body to believe that I am different than Lathsamy, that what happened to her could not possibly happen to me. Every day I catalog the differences. Lathsamy was trafficked, I had a single perpetrator. She was displaced and displaced again, lost her home, her family, her village, her culture, her language. I didn't lose any of these things. I have my parents, for all their uncountable flaws. I am trying to make friends with the wild child in me, the raging eight year old. I have unlocked the dungeon or she busted out, and either way I have invited her up into the clear light of day and I am trying to hold her, to make a safe space for her feelings, trying to do for myself what I failed to do for Lathsamy, for Lulu.

But I know there are no guarantees that the differences will prevail. It's not that I would follow Lathsamy's trajectory, I would find my own way to fall apart. The point is that it could happen, despite everything I understand about myself and everything I do to try to make myself whole. I need to look squarely at all the possibilities. No, not need to, I choose to. I could go into a post-partum depression, and if I do, then what? What if I become suicidal? What if something manic in me is unleashed? I am doing this as a single woman and if the strain or stress or hormones or mysteries of becoming a mother overpower me, what becomes of the child?

I have had long conversations with Hannah. I asked her to be the one to take care of my child if I shatter, and she has agreed. It could be for a month, it could be for the duration, it may never need to happen, and that of course is what we hope but there is no way of knowing, and in the face of not knowing I have a plan instead of just hoping for the best and paving the way for disaster. We have needed to talk through a lot of hard things. I asked what would happen if her marriage ended, would she be willing to take on being a single mom. Or if she and her husband had kids of their own by then and she got saddled with another one. We talked about the amount of time and care and love she will need to put into being part of my child's life from day one, so if she does need to take over she is already family for the child. We struggled with what would happen if we disagreed about whether I was able to care for my child, and what we came up with was that we would do our best to listen to each other and put egos aside and make a wise decision together.

Hannah brought up George, and honestly I didn't even want to think about him, let alone talk about him; but she pointed out that regardless of my feelings he could have legal standing as the child's biological father and if she is going to be the fallback parent in the event of my becoming incapacitated, the last thing she needs is for George to show up out of the blue and claim parental rights. What could I say? Of course she's right and it's an issue I have to face up to. What if I'm walking down the street with my child and I run into him? I really don't think it's going to happen, he lives across the river in Jamaica Plain and I could go a whole lifetime never running into a single person I know who lives in Jamaica Plain—but it's not impossible. What happens when my child is old enough to ask about her or his father? Or if the child wants contact with him? I wish these questions didn't exist and I am not ready to start making decisions, but I know I will have to and I've made a commitment to Hannah that we will keep talking about George.

So Hannah and I have a plan, and it's not finished and it won't ever be perfect but I think it will be enough. Of course this plan of ours is not only to do with me getting too depressed or too psychotic to function. I could get cancer, or MS, or lupus, or you name it. I could walk out the door one morning and be hit by a car. These things do happen. We always think they won't happen to us, but sometimes they do. A woman in my neighborhood was out riding her bike a few weeks ago and was hit by a truck and killed. One minute she was living her everyday life and the next minute she was dead.

But these are freak events. How likely am I to be hit by a car and leave my child behind? How likely to come down with a devastating disease? Or a crushing episode of mental illness. How much am I risking by going through with this and having a child? What are the odds? I don't think it matters. I'm not making a bet. I'm making a choice. I'm choosing life.

Okay, let's get some stuff straight. For starters, I'm going to keep saying fuck as much as I want, and that right there tells you a lot about how much I haven't changed and don't plan to change. Yeah, right, that Jane lady tells me not to say fuck you and maybe I do go along when I'm in her fucking office, but she can't control what goes on inside me and in my head I can say fuck you whenever I please. Fuck you Fuck you Fuck you Fuck you Fuck you.

Here's another thing. Just because Big Becky remembers all this stuff, just because she cries real tears and tells Mark to go fuck himself and does whatever she does with our mother and writes in her whoopdedoo journal and goes to see that Jane lady and makes like everything is different, everything is not different. For me nothing is fucking different, I do not forget and I do NOT forgive, not any of them, not Mark, not Mom, not our fucking father, and especially not the FB. Thirty years in the dungeon and now I'm supposed to say everything is roses? Give me a fucking break. Okay, so she's doing stuff I never thought she would do, but so what? It's not like I'm going down on my knees and kissing her toenails just because after all this time she comes to her senses and notices that I actually exist and I'm the one who carries every bad thing that ever happened to us on my fucking back, and now she finds it in the goodness of her heart to say, oh by the way, you down there, you don't look so hot. No, I don't look so hot, and I don't feel so hot.

Now she's gone and decided to have a baby. It's pretty disgusting if you ask me, I mean don't expect me to be getting up in the middle of the night to change any gross diapers. And breast feeding—I'm eight years old! If she tries to drag me into this mothering stuff there will be hell to pay, the last thing I'm about to do is be a mother.

Well, maybe a big sister. I don't know about right away, I mean babies are pretty boring and when they're not being boring they're being gross with all that pooping and spitting up and they cry way too much. But later on, when she's three or four and I can play dolls with her, and house, and we can bake cookies and read books and draw and paint and I get to show her all this stuff because I'm older and bigger and smarter. That might not be so bad. And anyone tries to hurt her, they better watch the fuck out for me because they will not know what hit them. And oh yeah, it better be a girl.

One thing is for sure, after the baby is born she better not forget about me, the FB. I can hear the excuses already, the baby kept me up and I'm too tired, I don't have time for the journal today, the baby is sick, the baby is hungry, the baby is cranky, the baby this the baby that and the baby always comes fucking first. Well I'm not going back down without a fight. The FB may be bigger and stronger but I have a voice and I can scream louder than any baby on this planet.

So I'm going to admit some stuff. Are you ready for this? I like being out of the dungeon. I like the fucking journal, whatever I said about it before. I like it that she keeps showing up every day and talks to me. I like the attention. Okay, satisfied?

Just remember this. It doesn't make everything okay. It doesn't make anything okay. So don't give me any of that happy ending crap. You know, Big Becky wakes up and remembers stuff and gets all her shit together and makes nice to little becky and has her sweet little baby and they all live happily ever after. I do NOT live happily, not for a single second of a single minute of a single hour of a single day of my life.

It's like so much has changed and not a fucking thing has changed. I don't get it. If you asked me do I want to go back down to the dungeon, I'd say what? are you out of your fucking mind? It's like it matters a lot, being up here on the surface, and it doesn't matter one single bit.

You know how at the end of *The House at Pooh Corner* it

says Wherever they go and whatever they do there, in the enchanted spot at the top of the forest a boy and his bear are always playing? Well that's how it is with me, except for me it says Wherever they bladdy blah and whatever they bladdy blah, in that spot on the floor of her room a girl will always be getting fucked by her big brother. I know that sounds pathetic and maybe it is, but I'm not looking for pity, that's the last thing in the world I want. I'm only saying it because it's the fucking truth.

Acknowledgments

Lisa Pliscou has been my rock. She was with me every step of the way through successive drafts and gave me thoughtful, incisive feedback that helped to shape and reshape each aspect of the story. Above all she has believed in my writing. Without Lisa's support I doubt that this novel would have made its way into print, and certainly not in its current form.

My son, Eric Sluyter, took time from his very busy life to read my first draft and then to have a deep conversation which informed my first round of revisions. I am also grateful to Eric for introducing me to the recording of a Dharma talk given by Thich Nhat Hanh which inspired my conception of Becky's unfolding relationship with her child self.

Adam Sacks, Lydia Eccles, and Miki Kashtan read the novel at various stages of completion, and I am grateful to all of them for their suggestions and support. Joanna Marshall's suggestions played a key role in the final set of revisions that brought the novel to its current form. Monica Raymond gave me advice for a previous, unpublished novel that proved invaluable in the writing of this one.

I could not ask for a better editor than Betsy Delmonico. Her grasp of the broad scope of the story, her lively interest in the psychology of the characters, her keen attention to detail, and her generous affirmations of my writing have all made the process of bringing the novel into final form a joy.

"In the Present: 9/11" is a previously unpublished poem by Elisabeth Morrison.

The sensibilities that I brought to the writing of *The Therapy Journal* have been influenced by the full spectrum of my life experience. I am grateful to friends, family, partners, teachers, therapists, writers, co-workers, clients, allies and adversaries from whom I have learned about trauma, recovery, grief, the abuse of power, the sharing of power, social justice and injustice, violence and nonviolence, mindfulness, empathy, struggle, and acceptance.

I have published two essays which may be of interest to readers who would like to know how some of my personal background informed the writing of this novel. "Erving and Alice and Sky and Elisabeth" includes an account of my marriage to Elisabeth Morrison, from whose life I have transposed Lathsamy's story. The essay is available in print in *The Cincinnati Review* volume 12.2, Winter 2016; and online in the *Erving Goffman Archives* at *http://cdclv.unlv.edu/ega/articles/wineman_eg_ag_sg_16.pdf.* The last section of "Voice Lessons: Six Meditations on Language and Authenticity" describes the process through which I inhabited Becky Hoffman's voice, and the transposing of my own relationship with my mother into Becky's relationship with Leah. It is online in the journal *Catapult* at *https://catapult.co/stories/voice-lessons-six-meditations-on-language-and-authenticity.*

Donation of Royalties

All royalties from sales of this book are being donated to The Gatehouse, a Toronto organization providing support to individuals impacted by childhood sexual abuse; the Boston Area Rape Crisis Center, committed to ending sexual violence through healing and social change; and Bay Area Nonviolent Communication in Oakland, CA, which works to create a world where everyone's needs matter and people have the skills to make peace.

About the Author

(Photo by Terry Signaigo)

Steven Wineman is the author of two books of nonfiction, *Power-Under: Trauma and Nonviolent Social Change* (self-published at *www.TraumaAndNonviolence.com*, 2003) and *The Politics of Human Services* (South End Press, 1984). His essays and fiction have appeared widely in literary magazines. He is a survivor of childhood trauma, and a lifelong proponent of nonviolence and social equality. Steve retired in 2014 after working in community mental health for 35 years. He can be contacted at *steven.wineman@gmail.com*, welcomes comments about *The Therapy Journal*, and is available for author readings in the Boston area and elsewhere as travel logistics permit.

CPSIA information can be obtained
at www.ICGtesting.com
Printed in the USA
FFOW02n1408010917
39373FF